Herries
LAKELAND

The pack horse bridge at Wasdale Head with Great Gable beyond

Walking with a Camera in
Herries
LAKELAND

TREVOR HAYWOOD

FOUNTAIN
PRESS

To Tracy Dawn Haywood

and Les Badham

Published by
Fountain Press Ltd.
45 The Broadway
Tolworth, Surrey
England

ISBN 0 86343 023 6

Design and Layout by Grant Bradford
Typeset in Leamington Roman
Print Production by
Landmark Production Consultants
Printed and Bound by
Mateu Cromo Artes Graficas S.A. Spain

CONTENTS

Gathering reeds near Friars Crag Derwentwater

Author's Preface

There has always been a strong tradition of the regional in British fiction, Thomas Hardy's reorganised Dorset becomes the landscape of 'Wessex' in many of his novels, and it is impossible to think of Emily Bronte's 'Wuthering Heights' without conjuring up images of the wild and romantic Yorkshire moorland that provides its backdrop.

Hugh Walpole's great Cumberland saga the *Herries Chronicle*, while not regarded as 'classical' fiction, certainly belongs with these in his vivid evocation of English family life in the rugged Cumberland of the eighteenth and nineteenth centuries.

The four novels, *Rogue Herries, Judith Paris, The Fortress* and *Vanessa,* written between 1928 and 1932, are still in print, and are still widely read fifty odd years after their first appearance, a fitting testament to the remarkable fusion between fiction and landscape which Walpole achieved. After his move to Derwentwater in 1924 Walpole travelled widely in the western and northern fells, and by a mixture of driving and walking built up a mental catalogue of exciting locations that he could draw on later as a setting for Herries adventures. The novels are thus replete with stunning descriptions of the Lakeland area within a twelve mile radius of Keswick, and many of the villages, woods and fells there formed both the backdrop and the detail for the stories. The names of places and features in the landscape were rarely changed, although one or two houses spring up where there were none to be found.

The Herries family reached both high and low in Walpole's fiction and this book follows in their footsteps. It provides background information on places used in the novels, it details a number of interesting walks and viewpoints, and it suggests ways in which the walker-photographer can make the most of this highly photogenic and unpredictable landscape. Keswick and Borrowdale are always popular with visitors to the Lakes; for those who would like to link an interest in walking and photography with the landscape used by Hugh Walpole in his Herries novels, this book is intended as a convenient guide.

I hope that you enjoy using it as much as I have enjoyed putting it together.

Trevor Haywood   *Kidderminster, January 1986*

The Birth of a Saga

Hugh Walpole came to live in the Lake District in 1924, at the age of 40, when he bought a Cumberland stone cottage, Brackenburn, some six miles from Keswick on the south western shore of Derwentwater.

He was enchanted with the spot immediately on seeing it, "a little paradise on Cat Bells" (his journal, November, 1923), and bought the house at once without the benefit of surveyors' reports or other formalities.

It had been built fifteen years earlier in a small hollow on the lower slopes of Cat Bells above Manesty Wood, and looked out across Derwentwater towards Skiddaw and Castlerigg Fell.

It was in this house, and much inspired by this view, that the great saga of the Herries family gradually took shape.

In many ways Hugh Walpole was two people. The gay raconteur and lion of the London literary and social set, needing to be liked, enjoyed being feted, desperately afraid that he might miss something; and the natural story teller, at peace with his art, loving the landscape, and deeply immersed in his work at the side of Derwentwater.

His was a sharply divided personality which craved, alternately, solitude and society, a division somewhat reinforced by his purchase, almost simultaneously with Brackenburn, of a lease on a batchelor flat at No 90 Piccadilly, at the corner of Half Moon Street, in January 1924. However, Walpole could never write very much in the midst of London, and as Brackenburn was seven hours away by car, careful timetabling became necessary, if both socialite and working author were to successfully co-exist.

The Herries Chronicles owe their origin to the success of this co-existence, to Brackenburn itself, and to the rugged Cumberland landscape that unfolded before Walpole's study window above Derwentwater.

As early as 28 August 1925, he noted in his diary a debt that he wanted to repay:-

> "I'm now pinning all my hopes to two or three Lakes novels, which will at least do something for this adorable place. I feel a longing desire to pay it back for some of its goodness to me."

His many other projects, however, made for a long gestation period, and his 'longing desire' had to wait until the end of May 1927 before he could begin to flesh-out his Cumberland thoughts.

It would be set in the eighteenth century, it would be called *Rogue Herries*, and it would be a ". . . fine queer book in the big manner. These four books shall clinch my reputation or I'll die in the attempt."

Despite various distractions, including his first insulin injection in early January, for the diabetes that had been diagnosed at the end of 1925, *Rogue Herries* was finished on 11 January 1929.

The next volume, tentatively called 'Lovers Under Skiddaw', but later changed to *Judith Paris*, was immediately allocated a slot in the 'work-in-progress' space of his fertile mind, along with an idea, not quite fulfilled as it turned out, of another epic series of novels taking the history of the Herries clan from Elizabethan times up to the point where *Rogue Herries began in 1730.*

The first words of Judith Paris were written on 5 September 1929. Soon after beginning his new novel, Walpole spent a day picnicking with his brother Robin and his sister Dorothea at the picturesque hamlet of Watendlath, just above the bridge at Ashness. The idyllic location of this small huddle of cottages and farmhouses, reflected in the small egg-shaped tarn below the Watendlath fells, ensured that it should play an important part in the turbulent life of Judith Paris, the passionate heroine of this second part of his grand design which was duly completed on 17 October 1930.

As usual, the end of one project signalled the beginning of another, and *The Fortress* was duly started at his sister's house in Edinburgh, on Christmas Eve, 1930, the third anniversary of the first words of *Rogue Herries*.

Judith Paris was published, with a dedication to J B Priestley, on 28 August 1931.

Walpole had met Priestley in September 1925 and they had become firm friends. In 1927 they had collaborated on a novel in the form of letters exchanged between two friends, *Farthing Hall*. The success which Walpole's name brought to this light gothic fantasy gave Priestley the economic security that he needed to concentrate on a big novel; it became *The Good Companions*, and he dedicated it to Hugh Walpole. Priestley survived his friend by 43 years and became a grand old man of English letters. He died in August 1984, (the centenary year of Hugh Walpole's birth).

On publication, *Judith Paris* sold well and was very popular. Priestley himself preferred her character to that of Rogue Herries, and the supposed house at Watendlath where she lived with Georges Paris became a popular pilgrimage for others who shared his view, encouraging the idea perhaps that Walpole's characters had actually existed in these locations, and that there really was such a place as 'Herries Lakeland'.

Walpole had later to settle a dispute in 1937 between two householders at Watendlath who both claimed that they lived in Judith Paris's house. Adopting something of the sagacity of Solomon, he revealed that in actual fact he had not based her house on any one building in the hamlet. No doubt the two litigants saw fortunes dwindle at the instant of this declaration.

Despite the author's undoubted authority for this, there is still a house at Watendlath today that carries a sign clearly marked 'The Home of Judith Paris'.

After the publication of *Judith Paris* many motor coach companies took parties of visitors around Derwentwater and unloaded them close to Walpole's house, the 'home of the celebrated author of the Herries novels', and in June 1932, he noted in his journal:

> "I am being pestered here by visitors who peer into my windows, invade my garage, discuss my books loudly and so on."

Hugh Walpole and J.B.Priestley at Brackenburn

Despite the 'charabanc' hordes, his ideas for *The Fortress* proceeded apace - more so after a drive with a friend early in 1931 out past Bassenthwaite Lake brought him to High Ireby and a Victorian house with large overgrown gardens and ornamental pools.

This seemingly empty and ramshackle mansion took him completely by surprise. It was strangely just as he had imagined Walter Herries' great gothic manor to be. Overlooking Uldale, it was the perfect symbol of the great Herries feud, and the struggles that came with it, it would become *The Fortress*.

Some locations were even more easily come by. Towards the end of *The Fortress*, Walpole causes Judith's son Adam Paris to build and live in a cottage on Cat Bells. This was in essence

'Brackenburn'. Walpole had only to look up from his desk to see the world as Adam Paris and his daughter Vanessa would see it. Such links as these, both physical and spiritual, between the author himself and the characters that he created in his Herries novels generated considerable emotional tension for Walpole.

When he walked out onto the hills and fells around his house, he walked in the footsteps of an extended family entirely of his own creation, whose innermost secrets he alone knew. They became companions, deeply real and close to him, and as each of their stories came to an end, it always left him with a feeling of emptiness and grief. The last words of *The Fortress* were completed after an almost solid eight-hour writing stint, on 1 November 1931.

At the end of 1931 Walpole felt pleased with the progress that he was making. He had completed three-quarters of his great project and he took the opportunity to read *Rogue Herries*, *Judith Paris* and *The Fortress* again and as a consequence noted in his journal:-

> "Old-fashioned they certainly are —
> verbose, over-emphasised, unreal in many
> places, sometimes very dull. But they are
> something
> — they have caught something definite out
> of both this place and me, and I think that
> people who come up here will read one or
> another of them for a while to come . . .

As with *Rogue Herries* and *The Fortress*, Walpole waited until Christmas Eve to begin the last of his Cumberland quartet, and the first words of *Vanessa* were written at Edinburgh on 24 December 1931.

Driven, perhaps, by his enthusiasm to complete the saga that had been his major preoccupation for five years now, Walpole dashed off seventy-five thousands words of *Vanessa* in the first two months of 1932, and the last pages were finished on 26 October of the same year.

His compact with Cumberland was now complete, readers of his Herries novels all over the world, saw this small portion of England through his eyes, and many of his own countrymen,

convinced of their authenticity, would come and seek out Herries names on tombs and gravestones, search for Herries houses in villages and towns, and shadow Herries ghosts along rivers and fells.

For his many thousands of readers, Walpole had successfully welded reality and imagination within a landscape that they could visit and identify with. The great enterprise that he once thought would take him at least ten years had been finished in just under five.

According to this plan, the next Herries tale was planned for 1939, it would have an Elizabethan setting and was tentatively entitled *Knights of the Queen*.

During October 1937 Walpole noted down in his journal the rough outline for such a work, and in July 1938 while staying at the Abbey Hotel, Malvern, for his annual visit to the Malvern Festival, he began writing *The Trumpet and Alarm*; this soon became *The Bright Pavilions*.

The fifth Herries novel took sixteen months to complete, (it was finished on 23 October 1939), and it centred on the tensions between Elizabeth I and Mary, Queen of Scots. Again, much of the action is set in Cumberland, including a witches' meeting at Watendlath, a visit to the German miners in the Vale of Newlands, and a reconstruction of their settlement on Derwent Island on Derwentwater.

The Bright Pavilions was published five months later in September 1940; this was the last Herries novel that Walpole would complete, and the last book that he would ever see published.

In the plan that he sketched out in 1934, Walpole had set aside 1942 for *Herries Moon, a Charles I/ Civil War Herries which would follow straight on the Elizabethan novel. He was working on this story, renamed Katherine Christian* when he died; what there was of it was published in 1944.

He had begun this in August 1940, and continued to write it, in fits and starts, at Brackenburn, interrupted by his failing health and his increasingly stressful visits to bomb-torn London.

The two other Herries stories that Walpole set out

Brackenburn: Walpoles' house on the South West edge of Derwentwater. Walpole wrote much of his Herries Chronicle in his study above the garage on the left of the photograph.

in his 1934 plan were, for 1943, *Men Under Skiddaw*, a James II and William III Herries, and, for 1944, *Death of Queen Anne's Men*, a Queen Anne Herries, the last words of which would lead directly on to the beginning of *Rogue Herries*.

These last two were never to get past the 1934 plan. During March 1936 Walpole indulged in yet another bout of (as it turned out totally unfulfilled) Herries planning. He contemplated writing another six Herries novels that would take the history of the family on from *Vanessa* up to the 1950s.

Hugh Walpole was fifty-seven when he died. Had he lived another ten years or so, it is almost certain that he would have completed *Katherine Christian*, and probably a seventh and eighth Herries story taking the saga on from where *Katherine Christian* would then have ended to the beginning of *Rogue Herries*.

The seal was really set on Hugh Walpole's 'Herries' achievement in May 1939, when Harold Macmillan suggested to him that Macmillan should publish the four Herries novels in one volume as the *Herries Chronicle*. This gave Walpole great pleasure and the 1,488 pages of text with a new foreword was duly published in October of the same year. It was an instant success with 60,000 copies being sold before publication, and Macmillan expecting to sell another 40,000 before Christmas.

It is this edition of the four Herries novels which is perhaps the easiest to turn up as a bargain in second-hand bookshops today.

The arrival of an advance copy of this handsome

volume for Walpole's own inspection proved momentous for him. He noted in his journal:-

> "... nearly a million words for 8/6 — and I do believe that for many years to come visitors to the Lakes will look at some part of it, if only because there are here the real names of local places. It carries the English novel no whit further but it sustains the tradition and has vitality".

Vitality it certainly had! The heroic scale and enormous continuity of family and location allowed Walpole's natural gifts as a storyteller to range over a broad canvas.

This was his most personal project and in it he succeeded in re-creating something of the fullness and substantiality of vision that was the traditional English novel. Not a work of genius or great psychological insight, but a powerful evocation of time and place still enjoyed by readers seeking a good story amid the wild romance of the Cumbrian landscape.

Hugh Walpole died at Brackenburn on the morning of Whit Sunday 1 June 1941 after a diabetic coma had proved too much of a strain for his heart. He is buried beneath a Celtic cross in the churchyard of St John's, Keswick, at a spot that he had chosen some years earlier, overlooking Derwentwater and Cat Bells in the midst of the land he had given to the Herries and through them to thousands who had never seen it..

Commemorative plaque to Walpole set in a rock at his favourite spot just above Brackenburn.

Sources

Hugh Walpole
'The Herries Book', a MSS notebook kept by Walpole outlining some of the major themes to be covered by the novels, and noting dates, ages, and Herries family pedigrees, is very useful in showing his development of ideas and characters in the novels, and is available for inspection on application to the Curator, at the Fitzpark Museum, Keswick.

Hugh Walpole
Bound MSS copies of all the Herries novels, also found in the Fitzpark Museum, Keswick.

Hugh Walpole
The novels *Rogue Herries* (1930), *Judith Paris* (1931), *The Fortress* (1932) and *Vanessa* (1933), first published separately by Macmillan, and later in 1939 in one volume as *The Herries Chronicle*, are the main source for locations: The novels are still available from Pan Books.

Sir Rupert Hart-Davis's
Excellent and detailed work, 'Hugh Walpole: A Biography', published in 1952, by Macmillan and reprinted in paperback by Hamish Hamilton in 1985, is the main secondary source for material on Walpole's life, and includes valuable extracts from the author's diaries and journals. All quotations from Walpole's journal are taken from this.

Elizabeth Steel's
'Hugh Walpole', published by Twayne Publishers Inc (USA), in 1972, includes some very useful analyses of Walpole's work and contemporary standing.

Marguerite Steen's
'Hugh Walpole: A Study', published by Ivor Nicholson and Watson in 1933, just after Walpole had completed *Vanessa* suffers from its unmitigated hero-worship, but does provide some very useful information about actual Herries locations.

Walking with a Camera

The beauty, variety, isolation and constantly changing light of the Lake District has attracted photographers long before cameras were really portable. In the 1890s, equipped with heavy wooden plate cameras and equally heavy tripods and accessories, mountain photographers such as the Abraham brothers of Keswick linked walking and climbing with photography to bring back the first photographs of some of the wildest locations in Lakeland. More recently the intrepid W.A. Poucher's pioneering work with the 35mm format since 1930 has done much to encourage and inspire serious photography on the fells.

Today many of the visitors to this compact corner of England bring cameras of all shapes and sizes intent on simply recording what they see, taking a few family snaps among the peaks, or determined to capture a definite view of a particular scene.

Whatever their aim, walking with a camera in 'Herries' country offers the opportunity to photograph some exceptional landscapes via a network of paths and tracks which are easily accessible and generally not too exhausting.

I would like to emphasise that the present writer was no great walker, or 'natural man of the fells', and although now thoroughly addicted to walking in the Lakes, the whole experience was quite new to me. I have had to walk to get many of the photographs that I wanted but I have not overtaken many people in the process.

That said, I have had some quite exhilarating moments, seen some of Nature's more amazing lighting set-ups and met some wonderful people. Once or twice I would have traded all my photographic equipment for just one helicopter ride home, but these occasions were rare and usually to do with rain.

Who you go walking with, and how many of you go, is a matter for personal taste and organisation. Sometimes friends came with me to the higher places and I was grateful for their companionship and help. This means that they could carry some equipment and enabled me to take both a 35mm and a larger (645) format outfit with me, slightly broadening the range and size of pictures that I could take. When I walked on my own, an equally exhilerating experience, I took only the 35mm equipment, as the weight of both this and the larger format gear meant that I wouldn't have got much above the 1,000 foot mark, let alone to Scafell Pike. Once or twice I did take both sets of equipment when I walked on my own, but only to small peaks like Cat Bells and Castle Crag, and there are grooves in my shoulders to prove it.

At this point it is probably timely to note that many of the photographs in this book were not taken on the high fells, they were taken at road or lake level. There are lots of interesting pictures to be taken in 'Herries Land' just by driving to some key points and then walking on tarmac roads or low level tracks, clicking off some very nice pictures on the way. Derwentwater and the fells around it, Borrowdale, the Vale of Newlands, the Castlerigg Stone Circle, Grange, and views of Skiddaw and Blencathra are good examples of features that cry out to be photographed just a few yards from a car door, and are none the less spectacular or satisfying for that.

Obviously some features only exist on the tops and so you have to climb. Also many features available at road level look completely different from higher up and so the range and variety of your landscape photography is much enhanced by being prepared to hoof it up well-worn tracks to some of the famous tops.

What to Wear?

Everywhere in the lakes there are books and posters telling you what to wear when fell walking, how to get properly prepared and what to do if you hit any trouble. Read some of these and take your pick; my aim was to be comfortable and to be prepared for extremes of rain and cold. Everyone has strong personal preferences when it comes to walking gear and the views that I canvassed varied from shorts and trainers to full Alpine kit, eventually I settled on the following:-

Great Gable, Green Gable and Styhead Tarn

All Seasons

Light, waterproof walking boots, thick, long socks with as much wool in them as possible. A bright red rucksack on a light plastic frame with side and front pockets, size 18" x 6".

Spring/Summer

Light shirt and shorts, with a thick military-type pullover, waterproof jacket and trousers in the rucksack.

Autumn/Winter

Cord trousers (avoid denim as it almost doubles its weight when wet) thick check shirt, thick military pullover, and if it is winter, a pair of extremely warm longjohns. Again, I carried a waterproof jacket and trousers in the rucksack.

Obviously there may be better permutations for you, and comfort generally comes with experiment and experience. I stick to walking boots in all seasons because my feet need support, and because the terrain across the whole district is often wet or boggy even at the height of summer. The 'trainer' set would not agree and in the end you must sort it out for yourself.

Weather

Whatever your inclination when you start out on a walk, bear in mind that the weather here is some of the most unpredictable in the world, and that if it should rain when you are high up and five miles from your car or the nearest bus stop it will be a miserable walk back without some sort of waterproof covering.

I tended not to walk to high places if it was already misty or raining at the point from where I was going to start.

There is no absolutely reliable weather forecasting for the tops, although just like everyone else, I took note of what the local weather men said, added this to what I found and how I felt when I got to my start point, and decided what to do there and then, like everyone else I had mixed success but was probably luckier than most.

Some mist and dark cloud can add mood and power to landscape photographs so dark days shouldn't always be dismissed out of hand. However, thick mist and rain settling in at a low point of departure is unlikely to mean that it will be any better higher up; it's probably worse and the good pictures are somewhere else.

If you plan to walk to some of the higher locations suggested in this book you would be wise to leave a message with someone at your base telling them where you are going and when you expect to be back. Another useful precaution is to write a note of your intended destination, slip it into a plastic cover and place this under the windscreen wipers of your car if it is parked near your point of departure.

I appreciate that this all seems a bit dramatic just for a day's walking, but it is a fact that large numbers of very sensible people get stuck on the fells every year as a result of an accident or suddenly worsening weather conditions or both, and these quite simple precautions can aid those who might have to locate you in an emergency.

Having sounded the warning note many of the walks included in the following sections are low-level walks that can be completed in two or three hours depending on your rate of walking, and how often you stop to take photographs.

As well as sensible clothing and an intelligent appreciation of the weather conditions, a good day's walking is much enhanced by a bit of

Scafell Pike and Scafell from Wastwater

planning. A must for this is the relevant sections of the Ordnance Survey's 1:25,000 (Yellow Covers) Outdoor Leisure Maps of the English Lakes. There are four of them, and although not precisely covering the extremities of the Herries Landscape, the N.W and S.W. sheets cover 80% of the Herries compass.

For the northern area around High Ireby, Uldale, Caldbeck, Hesket Newmarket and the 'back o' Skidda' you will need Sheet 90 Penrith and Keswick of the O.S. 1:50,000 (Pink Covers) Landranger series. Sheet 89 West Cumbria is also useful giving complete coverage of the area between Keswick and the coast.

The O.S. 1 inch Lake District Tourist Map (illustrated cover) showing part of the National Park boundary is useful for its impression of the whole area, and for its special shading which gives the mountains and valleys a distinctly three dimensional appearance.

By spending some time with a map, and by always taking a map with you, (you can buy a clear plastic map holder for use when walking, quite cheaply from any of the equipment shops in the area), you can sort out precisely where you want to go, how you are going to get there and the features to look at along the way, and, how long it is likely to take you.

Provisions

There is not usually room for gourmet meals in the average rucksack and each walker will have a very personal approach as to how much, and what should be included as sustenance along the way. My advice is that on long walks taking the best part of a day, I needed quite a lot but then I eat too much anyway. Food has to juggle for space in the rucksack with clothing, cameras and lenses, film and filters, maps, and little things like a compass and a whistle (six distinct blasts for an emergency). Just remember that you might be burning calories up at a slightly faster rate than when taking pictures of the kids back at home.

Remember that people live and work among these mountains and valleys, so avoid leaving litter of any kind; always close gates behind you and never take dogs unless they are on a lead, especially during the spring lambing season. Frustrated farmers can shoot loose dogs on sight if they seem to be wandering around sheep without control.

19

Herries Walks
General Information

Beginning by Bus

Local bus and coach information is available from the Keswick Bus Station, Tithebarn Street, Telephone (0596) 72791.

A comprehensive bus timetable, including many services operating in the areas covered by this book, is available from Cumberland Motor Services, Head Office, Tangier Street, Whitehaven, CA28 7XF, Telephone (0946) 63222-3/4/5/6/7.

This office also has details of National Express Coach services to Cumbria from all parts of the country, as well as details of Explorer tickets, Day Rover Tickets, special holiday services etc., which, with some forward planning, can help cut the cost of your travel and make your arrangements simpler.

If you plan to use bus services in Cumbria ring the Whitehaven offices in advance of your visit, and they will send you all the information you need. **All numbered services noted in the text are those provided by Cumberland Motor Services Ltd.

Some useful services are offered in and around Herries country by the Mountain Goat Bus Company. Formed in 1972 this company uses rugged and manoeuvrable 12 seater mini buses, (Goats) to take visitors on whole or half day tours around the Lake District. Some of these include places noted in this book, and a full list of their tours is available from: The Mountain Goat Bus Co., Victoria Street, Windermere, Cumbria. Telephone (09662) 516.

They also have an office at the Queens Hotel, Keswick, Telephone (0596) 73962 which is manned from April to September. They also run services on a regular timetable from Keswick via Stair in the Vale of Newlands to the Fish Inn at Buttermere, and details of pick up points and times can be obtained from the above addresses.

Beginning by Car

If you are using a car you need little more than a map and good weather to set you up for some exciting exploration.

Remember however that there are no petrol stations away from the main centres of population, even some quite large villages will not have one, so fill-up in preparation for any long drives. The area covered in this book is quite compact and so this shouldn't pose too much of a problem.

Also remember that there are not many 'phone boxes at the bottom of mountains so ensure that your car is reasonably 'fit' before you start, and that it can cope with some steep hills, and that you can cope with plenty of bends and some very narrow roads.

You might remember not to park on the sides of narrow roads for long periods. As well as welcoming tourists, Cumbria is also keen to attract and retain industrial and commercial traffic, and eccentric roadside parking can cause serious difficulties for lorries and vans as well as buses and other holiday visitors.

There are plenty of roadside car parks and pull-ins near all the features mentioned in this book and so finding somewhere to park your car while you go walking should pose no real problems.

Weather Information

Lake District weather is frequently unpredicatable and can be the source of considerable disappointment and irritation, especially for photographers.

To help you organise your time and decide on appropriate clothing the National Park Authority operate a 24 hour weather service. Obviously their predictions about future conditions over certain fells and valleys has about as much success as any other source of weather forecasting and you should treat it as such. Too many forces are at work in the atmosphere over the higher fells to deal in certainties.

Telephone Windermere (09662) 5151 at any time.

The Helvellyn range from the gate below Skiddaw Little Man on Skiddaw

Borrowdale and Rosthwaite

A valley of many secrets, Borrowdale is certainly one of the most beautiful and compact areas in the Lakes, offering a tremendous variety of scenery among its volcanic crags and picturesque hamlets.

For the photographer and walker it offers a tapestry of changing light and shapes that would be difficult to find anywhere else in England. So compact is the valley that legend reports that the inhabitants once tried to build a wall across the valley to keep the cuckoo from leaving so that they would always have good weather. Their aim was understandable. Seathwaite, at the southern end of the valley, has some of the highest annual rainfall in England, and the gauges used to record this unhappy statistic are scattered all around the Seathwaite Fells; little wonder that some have called Borrowdale the 'Devil's Chamber Pot'.

Acquired by the monks of Furness Abbey in 1210, Borrowdale was host to early settlers well before this date, and many place names suggest a strong Norse influence. The most common element, 'thwaite', derives from an old Norse word for 'a clearing', and the name Borrowdale itself is probably of Norse origin, meaning 'valley of the fortress' - possibly a reference to Castle Crag, a wooded hill crowned with a prehistoric earthwork that blocks the Jaws of Borrowdale above Grange.

It is in this gentle valley that Hugh Walpole set the beginning of his great saga, and it provides the tapestry against which so much of the drama of *Rogue Herries* takes place. Here, where the comfortable Hazel Bank Hotel stands now, on a gentle rise above the stream Walpole set the wind-blown house of Herries.

Shut off under the fells and crags of Borrowdale, the old house that Walpole set here had been deprived of all civilised attention since the mid-sixteenth century. During that time it had been the home of an Elizabethan Herries, a favourite of the

Borrowdale and Rosthwaite from the path to Watendlath

Queen, who had come to Cumberland to survey the foreign miners at work around Keswick.

Here one dark and windy night in 1730, Francis 'Rogue' Herries brings his family at the beginning of Walpole's first Herries novel. In the eighteenth century before the slippery tracks gave way to proper roads the villagers of Borrowdale had to be self-sufficient. Cut off from the outside world for many months of the year, their muddy lives were despised by the 'Rogue's' elder brother Pomfret Herries, who preferred the marginally more civilised amenity of Keswick itself;

> "There's not a cart in Borrowdale, brother, nor a road to carry one. It's all horseback round here. Damn it, you're in Chiney in Borrowdale, but never say I didn't warn you. You wanted cheap living and you've got it. Naked bottom and bare soil! That's life in Borrowdale."

The warning is wasted, nothing can keep Rogue Herries from the deeps of Borrowdale.

Journeying from Keswick, by moonlight and on horseback, at the beginning of *'Rogue Herries'*, Francis Herries and his household skirt the edge of Derwentwater, through the gateway of high rock into the enclosed valley.

It is through the eyes of young David Herries that we get our first glimpse of the frugal house that is to be the dark centre of the family's life in Borrowdale.

The Hazel Bank Hotel, on the site of Rogue Herries house at Rosthwaite

"David looked at the house and was sadly disappointed. Under the black hills it seemed so very small, and in the white moonlight so cold and desolate. It appeared to be two houses: on the right it was high, with a gabled roof and thin latticed windows; then it dropped suddenly to a low rough-seeming building with shaggy farm byres at its hinder end".

Tucked for safety and shelter below Yew Crag the dark house and its surroundings begin to impress themselves on the Herries family. Some of its secrets were already known to Francis:

> "Beyond the fields, in far distance, this humped, lumpish hill, Glaramara, sprawled in the early morning light. Herries knew well its name. For so long as he could remember he had known precisely how this house must stand, and all its history."

This is the house where his long-suffering wife becomes ill and dies; where he will pit his body against the unyielding ground, where the mad marriage feast is held after the 'Rogue's' wedding to Mirabel Starr, and where his son David brings his own Sarah after the struggle by Sprinkling Tarn.

This is also the house where Judith Paris was born, as the snow piled up against the windows, and where both her mother, Mirabel Starr, and her father died at her birth:-

> "both dead in one hour".

From here Squire Gauntry took her up from her cot and carried her to Stone Ends.

In the subsequent novels the 'old house' is allowed to fall back into disrepair and eventually ruin. But its magnetism, its location, and its history are too strong for Walpole to let go. In *Judith Paris* he causes Judith and Warren Forster to ride out to Borrowdale, after a family disturbance at Uldale, they come to explore the place of her birth, now used as a shelter by a shepherd and his wife.

They make a fire and Judith soaks up the shades and shadows of her parents, her wild gypsy mother and her father, the infamous 'Rogue'. They make love among her memories and Adam Paris is

Castle Crag and the Jaws of Borrowdale from the Northern edge of Derwentwater

conceived in the same house as his mother.

In *The Fortress* the crippled Uhland also visits Rosthwaite, seeking links with his great-great-grandfather. He roams around the tumble-down house, sits on the stairs and imagines the old scarred Herries watching him.

The weeds will eventually consume and cover it, but it will not vanish, all the Herries need some part of it, to cherish, to remember, to rail against, the author cannot release it.

Today the Stonethwaite Beck still winds its way under the little bridge on its journey to the River Derwent, and to many who remember Walpole's stories, this is still a place of pilgrimage, fascination and recollection.

The many pathways and walks that skirt the valley and its tributaries open up a feast of opportunities for the walker and photographer and the modern visitor is soon at home among its wooded slopes and hamlets.

Not so the poet Thomas Gray. Arriving beneath Gowder Crag, during October 1769, the vision of the great volcanics towering above and before him reminded him too much of those places in the Alps where the guides recommend moving at speed and in silence, "less the agitation of the air should loosen the snows above, and bring down a mass that would overwhelm a caravan".

His apprehensions got the better of him, he peeped through the 'Jaws of Borrowdale' and beat a hasty retreat, never quite making it into the valley proper, leaving us a poetic fancy of the terrors that lay among the paths that led over the Sty Head Pass into Wasdale:

> ". . . that ancient kingdom of the mountaineers, the region of Chaos and Old night."

My own favourite view of this 'dreadful' place is from Castle Crag. Only 985 feet above sea level, this highly individual stump, the tooth in the Jaws of Borrowdale, is easy to climb and gives an excellent prospect of the valley and many of the famous fells to the south and south-west of it, particularly Great End and Glaramara. Looking north, Skiddaw, Blencathra, Derwentwater and nearby Grange all look as if you could reach out and touch them; in both directions the land of the Herries is reduced to Lilliput, dramatic confirmation that small really is beautiful.

How to get there

Maps

O.S. 1:25,000 (yellow cover) N.W. sheet, and O.S. 1:50,000 (pink covers) sheet 89 West Cumbria *or* sheet 90 Penrith and Keswick.

By Bus

Using service No. 79 the Keswick to Seatoller service alighting at Grange.

By Car

Along the B5289 south from Keswick to Grange, parking in the small car park by the bridge in the village or at some other suitable place off the road.

The Walk

Borrowdale and Rosthwaite

Walk through the village, past the tempting home-made smells of the Grange Bridge Cottage Restaurant, it was the Grange Post Office in Walpole's day, until you reach the cafe opposite the Grange Hotel. Turn left here down Hollows Lane and follow the signpost "Bridleway to Honister (Footpath to Hollows Farm)" along the tarmac road noting the wooded slopes of Greatend Crag and Grange Fell rising up above the Borrowdale road on your left and the rough lower crags of Maiden Moor on your right.

The white buildings of Hollows farm just above the grassy fields on your right signal a fork in the road, take the left fork down past the camping ground, the tarmac road now giving way to a more basic, but quite wide track.

Bear left along the side of the stone wall into the woods, down towards the river. A number of streams run into the Derwent here and after a heavy rainfall good waterproof footwear is necessary if you are to enjoy sploshing across them. Just off to your right you will see a wooden bridge crossing one of the wider streams, in summer you may well be able to walk across the dry river bed, but in winter the bridge comes into its own. There are some interesting views of the river through the trees and the woodland area on your right is Dalt Wood, home of the now disused quarry from which the stone was taken to build Brackenburn. The left-hand path follows the river bank to the stone bridge and stepping stones that lead to Rosthwaite.

If desired this route can be enjoyed on the return journey as an alternative to the longer road route which I suggest later, or it can be taken now, avoiding the diversion up to Castle Crag.

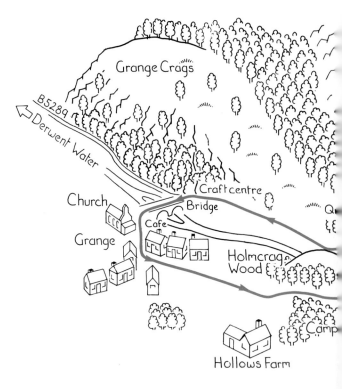

My advice however is to cross over the simple plank bridge, which covers part of a stream, indeed when the water here is in spate it hardly covers half of it, bearing off to the right along the wider stone path up through the wood signposted "Bridleway Seatoller, Honister" following this route alongside the beck, crossing the wooden bridge over on your right or just stepping gingerly over the stones in the stream which now moves over to your left.

Make your way through the gate and out of the wood looking out for the steeply wooded north face of Castle Crag just above an old stone-built sheep fold at its base. Take some time to admire the view north from here, dominated by Skiddaw which just seems to grow out of the lake and the meadows beyond Grange. This is a fine and unusual vantage point for some photography,

particularly if you can get a bit of height over the stone boulders that are strewn about here. Take the stone-slabbed bridge over the beck and continue up past the large boulders on your right. The precarious-looking spoil heaps of Castle Crag are now in evidence as a number of different paths up to the Crag present themselves.

Take the grassy slopes past the big cairn on your left walking up towards the dry-stone wall through which some stone steps give access.

Up on your right a wooden seat and a slate memorial to Sir William Hamer dated 1939, offer a pleasant stopping-off point before the climb through the spoil heaps to the summit. Although quite steep the path is easy to follow, over the wooden ladder against the stone wall, and the wooden stile over a wire fence, following the stone

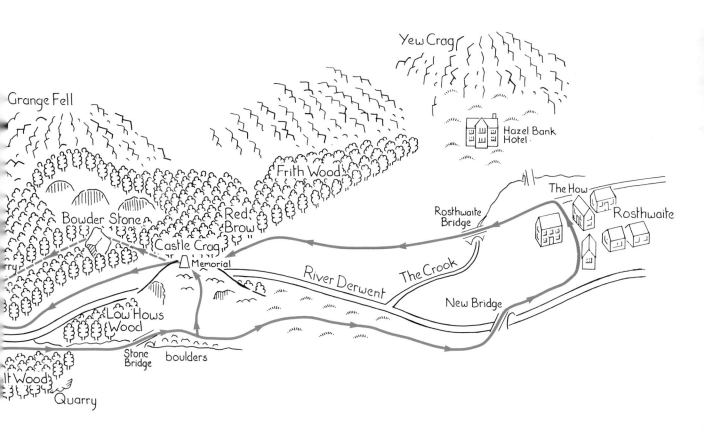

Looking South at Borrowdale from the summit of Castle Crag

and slate cairns that mark the route. Take care over the loose shale, and note the ever-present wall of Great End to the south, often capped by swirling mist and clearly signalled by the Grains Gill path directly below it. Make your way up the zig-zag route that has been cut through the spoil heaps on this side of the Crag. They look as if they could, at any minute, start slipping and sliding taking a few walkers with them, but no fatalities have been reported so they must be more firmly fixed than they look.

Rest a moment at the large slate-piled cairn just below the summit from which the village of Rosthwaite can be enjoyed in the lush valley below.

The last few yards to the summit, along the side of the old quarry workings, are an easy scramble bringing you out onto the grassy top surmounted by a memorial to men from this area who fell in the First World War.

Although not very high, the uninterrupted views in all directions, particularly north over Grange and Derwentwater to Skiddaw, and to the south over Borrowdale offer a spectacular panorama of Herries country.

Photographers will find plenty to fill their frames with up here, and there is a lot of space to move around for trying out different viewpoints and lenses.

Take the same route down, (there is only one), and aim for the wooden gate through the stone wall on your left just below the summit. This brings you onto a pleasant, woodland shale path that becomes quite steep in places and which eventually brings you out onto a gentle grassy track, through a wooden gate and over a small stone-slab bridge into the meadows of the Borrowdale valley alongside the River Derwent.

Soon you are at the lovely stone arch of New Bridge, you can cross the river here, or you can continue along the river side and chance the fine

Memorial on the summit of Castle Crag

stepping stones a little further on. Whichever you chose you will soon be on the path, between dry-stone walls that bring you into Rosthwaite.

Take some time to explore the interesting stone and whitewashed houses and farm buildings here, they are very attractive and often missed by car-bound visitors who speed through the eastern tip of the village.

Walk through the village, past the handy public conveniences and public phone box and turn left onto the road opposite the Post Office and general stores, and walk towards Keswick. After a few yards note the Hazel Bank Hotel on a grassy knoll past the little humped bridge on your right; this stands on the site that Hugh Walpole used for Rogue Herries' house in the first novel of the Herries saga, at the foot of Yew Crag, and at the centre of the valley that he made his own.

Strange as it may seem, this is a case where the valley can be savoured just as well from the road as from anywhere else, so enjoy the views, both north and south, and imagine the isolation and closeness of this community before a road was made through the "Jaws" in 1842. Until that time the pack-horse road from Keswick to Rosthwaite ran through Watendlath and down off the side of Brund Fell to Rosthwaite.

After about a mile or so the road moves into the narrows alongside the river between Castle Crag and Red Brow. Here you can leave the road if you wish to take the interesting riverside path that runs just below it half a mile or so into the Jaws of Borrowdale, or look out for the stile and gate on the right that will take you off the road and through the woods to the famous Bowder Stone. Set among Borrowdale Birch trees this 30 foot high rock is something of a puzzle, was it brought here by a glacier or did it just tumble off Bowder Crag?

The woodland path to the Bowder Stone

The Bowder Stone

Whatever the cause, here it is, 1,900 tons of it precariously balanced on what seems to be an impossible point of rock. Visitors have been attracted to it for well over two hundred years now, indeed in the late eighteenth century the eccentric Joseph Pocklington installed an old lady in a cottage nearby for the express purpose of shaking hands with tourists through a hole at the narrowest point of the stone.

After a quick run up the steps to see if it will fall over with your particular weight on it, continue your walk through the delightful wood, past the great slabs that rise out of the disused Quayfoot Quarry until you reach the road again.

Follow the road along the river, stopping to visit the fine Lakeland Craft Centre on your right before crossing the double-arched bridge back into Grange.

If you have time, and if you would like to see Grange, its bridges and the River Derwent from above, take the stile on your right just before the Craft Centre, and make your way up the gentle slopes of Grange Crags. The western ledges of this benign and wooded fell provide some interesting views over the village, although the photographer in search of some wide-angle shots from these perches may be frustrated by the abundant foilage in high summer and find it more rewarding to wait for the bare trees of winter.

This last point emphasises Borrowdale's attraction as a place for walkers and photographers in all seasons. Winter and autumn can be just as exciting as spring and summer. The autumn colours in Borrowdale at the beginning of November are a photographer's dream, the silence and starkness of the landscape in winter sometimes overwhelming.

The surprises of light and shadow, mountain and water are there to be discovered at every season; try them when all the crowds have gone away and the peace has returned.

A black horse in Borrowdale

Wastwater from near the youth hostel

Ravenglass and Wastwater

It is difficult to imagine that Ravenglass was once a major port and Roman fort. The great sand bar and mud flats, (peppered on the map with 'DANGER AREA'), that escort the River Esk over its last few yards to the sea now prevent all but small craft from entering the estuary, and an expert eye is needed to pick out the last remains of the Roman fort of Glanoventa near the railway line to the south of the town.

These remains are probably the finest Roman buildings to be found in the north of England, and represent a Roman bath-house, which was attached to the nearby fort, standing to the full height of its walls. During the twelfth century the Pennington family became Lords of the Manor at Ravenglass and actually lodged in the Roman bath-house until better accommodation was provided on the site of the present Muncaster Castle.

The town gained its charter in 1209, and no doubt benefited from the ease of access afforded from its eastern hinterland by the old Roman road that extended from Ravenglass, deep into the fells, past the great Roman fort at Hardknott in Eskdale and on to Ambleside. A less Roman but very enjoyable way to see the coastal fells of Eskdale is to travel on the 'Ratty' narrow gauge railway. Built to carry iron ore from Eskdale to the coast, it now carries cheerful holiday makers to and fro on the seven miles between Boot in Eskdale and Ravenglass. A few miles to the north-west of Ravenglass lies the quietest, the deepest, the wildest and, for me, the most romantic of all the lakes.

Only three miles long, and about half a mile wide, its dramatic setting among some of the highest and most famous of the western fells creates an illusion of much greater size. Its south-western edge is unique among the lakes for the almost sheer cascade of scree that drops dramatically into its 258 feet of water.

Sprinkling Tarn

Wastwater looks and feels like the work of nature, a long deep trough, gouged out by ice and filled by the rains long before man or his sheep roamed beside it.

In *Rogue Herries*, Walpole uses the desolate shores of Wastwater for the first and only time as the setting for a romantic kidnap.

From Scarf Hall, (probably a fictional name for the real Wasdale Head Hall Farm), hidden in the woods under Green Howe at the northern end of Wastwater, David Herries steals his new-found love Sarah from under the nose of an oppressive uncle and her erstwhile suitor. At night, and in great melodramatic style they leave the hall, skirt the end of the lake, and make their way through the little cluster of houses at Wasdale Head towards the foot of the pass below Great Gable which will take them up to the struggle by Sprinkling Tarn.

During the spring of 1737, in *Rogue Herries*, Francis Herries and his son David leave the house at Rosthwaite and ride over to Ravenglass to visit Francis' elder brother Harcourt:

> "Meanwhile, in this April month, Francis and his son David rode together to Ravenglass to stay for several nights, with brother Harcourt. They rode over the Stye Head Pass and down into Wasdale.
>
> By the Stye Head Tarn it was grim and desolate. This Tarn lies, an ebony unreflecting mirror at the foot of the Gavel - beyond it to the left, soft green ridges run to Esk Hause and the Langdales and lonely Eskdale."

They ride down into Wasdale, past the silent Wastwater and its precipitious screes, out past Santon Bridge to the meadowland before the town and soon over the cobbles into Ravenglass itself. Here during a night-time excursion along the estuary where the Esk, the Irt and the Mite join into one meandering stream, father and son quarrel and fight among the pools and mud flats, and come to a new understanding together on the sands at Ravenglass.

Today under the moonlight, or at sunset the wide expanse of the estuary at Ravenglass can look eerie, romantic or just plain desolate, depending on your mood, while to the north, the cooling towers of the nearby Sellafield atomic power station, puff out their steam in a down-to-earth reminder of how delicate a thing the landscape is in the hands of man.

How to get there

Maps

Outdoor Leisure Map O.S. 1:25,000 (yellow cover) S.W. sheet. This includes Ravenglass, and O.S. 1:50,000 (pink covers) sheet 89 West Cumbria, this includes Wastwater but excludes Ravenglass.

By Bus

Service No. 12 serves Ravenglass as part of the Whitehaven-Thornhill-Seascale-Millom route. There is no regular bus service to Wastwater or Wasdale Head.

By Car

If you are in Keswick or Borrowdale and want to get to Ravenglass and Wastwater you cannot

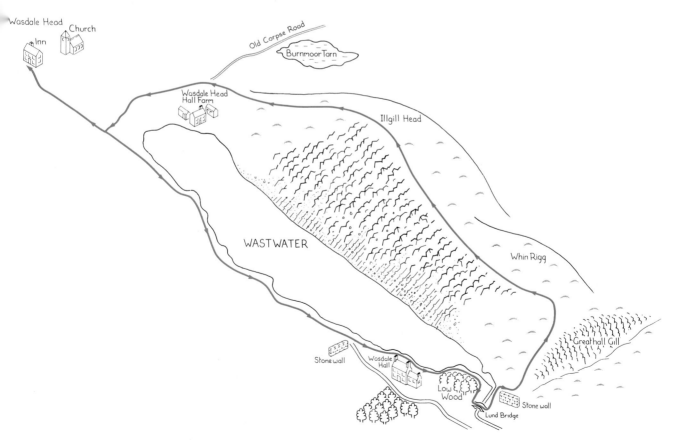

Wastwater from Whin Rigg

The estuary at sunset

avoid a long drive around the western fells as there are no motor roads between Seathwaite and Wasdale Head. There is of course a pleasant walk from Seathwaite over Sty Head and into Wasdale but this is quite a trek and you would have to walk back again. This walk is only tackled comfortably after an early start and with a full appreciation of the distances to be covered.

Ravenglass is reached off the A595 coastal road south of Seascale. There is a car park in the 'town' near the 'Ratty' and mainline railway stations and the one and only main street runs right on to the beach. At low tide the deserted mud flats are well worth exploring, sometimes brooding and eerie as banks of sea mist whisper across the phantom boats stranded on the sand, and sometimes host to the most spectacular sunsets.

Wastwater can be reached on a number of minor roads that wind inland from the A595. The road from Gosforth passes Walpole's childhood holiday haunt of Sowermyre Farm, before it drops down through Nether Wasdale, past the Youth Hostel to the south-western tip of the lake. The left fork in the road at Bengarth can also be taken. This approach offers a slightly more dramatic first sight of the crags above Wastwater and comes out at a point nearer to the centre of the lake.

There are plenty of car-parking places beside the lake for picnicking, or as a base for some lakeside exploration. Many fine walks spread out from Wastwater; on Yewbarrow, Lingmell and even Sca Fell itself, however none of these can, for me, compare with the breathtaking beauty of the landscape as seen from the ridge between Whin Rigg and Illgill Head directly above the Wastwater Screes.

Wastwater from Illgill

The Walks

Whin Rigg to Illgill Head starting from S.W. edge of Wastwater

Park your car off the road near the south-western end of Wastwater. Take the permitted path running through the grounds of the imposing Wasdale Hall built in 1829 and now a comfortable Youth Hostel leased from the National Trust. Accessed over a stile just off the edge of the lakeside road this interesting pathway passes right along the south-western tip of the lake and offers the opportunity for some spectacular photography. Looking back across the water with Great Gable as a brooding centrepiece at its northern end, there is plenty of scope for composition using all the focal lengths that you have available.

Continue on this path along the lakeside, through Low Wood, crossing Lund Bridge, over the stream that runs out of the lake eventually joining the River Irt on its way to the sea at Ravenglass. Now take the public footpath on the other side of the stream until arriving at a junction of two paths.

One path goes off left along the precarious base of the great Wastwater Screes, an interesting diversion for another day, but now take the right hand path, walking away from the lake for about

half a mile. This will take you alongside a gradually ascending wall until you reach the base of the great ravine which carries Greathall Gill. Keeping the ravine on your right follow the zig-zag route over the bracken, gradually moving off to the left, cutting the corner here, as you come to the gentle grassy slopes of Whin Rigg itself. Walk up to the cairn on Whin Rigg 1,755ft (535 metres), and prepare yourself for an exhilerating ridge-walk along the top of the screes. Have your camera ready; for the first half mile or so of this walk you will be spoilt for choice, the view-points, under the right conditions, are just fantastic. You will need to leave the main path and follow the edge of the escarpment as closely as possible if you are to avoid too much unnecessary foreground in your pictures, and if you are to take in the fascinating castellated shapes that rise out of the gullies and ravines that cut into the edge of the crumbling fellside. Those screes which looked so steep from the other side of the lake now seem much gentler as they slope away into the dark waters below.

On a clear day, you have magnificent views in all directions, particularly to the north over Yewbarrow, Kirk Fell and Great Gable, and to the west over the coastal plain to the sea, all changing slightly as you walk up to the cairns on Illgill Head, 1,983ft (609 metres).

The slopes just below and around the summit of Illgill are ideal places for a picnic before taking the path down off the top. This is quite steep at first as it moves from grass through heather to bracken,

Great Gable from Wasdale Head

Great Gable and Lingmell is a fascinating place, both for its highly photogenic scenery and also for the most amazing network of stone walls which generations of Wasdale farmers built to provide safety for their sheep, and just as important, to use up the vast quantity of stones that littered the valley floor. Attractive as this option is, bear in mind that you will eventually have to get back to your car at the south-western end of the lake, a walk of something like five and a half miles.

2.   The other option is to turn left on the tarmac road and walk the four miles or so back to your car. Following almost the whole length of the western shore of Wastwater this takes you directly opposite the high ridge that you walked over earlier and provides a clear view of the unique screes.

If you choose the second option you can of course drive back up to the Wasdale Head Inn for a look around, avoiding too much walking on made-up roads.

The coastal plane and Sellafield nuclear re-processing plant from Scafell Pike

and needs some care. As you come down, note Burnmoor Tarn off on your right, and the old 'corpse' road that runs past it across Eskdale Moor into beautiful Eskdale itself. At the foot of Illgill turn left on to the well-marked path that drops gently down above the northern head of Wastwater, just above the Wasdale Head Hall Farm. Disguised as Scarf Hall in *Rogue Herries*, this is where David Herries finds his bride, and from where they set out to face the fight in the fells above, near Sprinkling Tarn. On the right as you follow the path down towards the lakeside road the volcanic pillars of the Scafell range of fells rise out of the grassy slopes of Green How and Brown Tongue. In clear conditions a long telephoto lens can pick out some detail above Hollow Stones from here, although a position off the path, on the tarmac road itself, might provide a better viewpoint.

When you reach the road two choices are available:-

1.   Turn right and walk one and a half miles to the Wasdale Head Inn for some well-deserved refreshment. After about three-quarters of a mile there is a pleasant footpath on your left which takes you off the road and along a stream to the outbuildings at the back of the Inn. Near here also is the very pretty and very small Wasdale Head Church, with its climbers graves and small stained glass window featuring Napes Needle. The valley head here below Yewbarrow, Kirkfell,

The High Fells above Seathwaite

Seathwaite from the slopes of Glaramara

One and a quarter miles south-west of Rosthwaite, leaving the main road just before Seatoller, lies the little hamlet of Seathwaite.

A classic example of the tight cluster of farm houses that include 'thwaite' in their names, Seathwaite is known for its trout, its rain, and as a popular starting point for walkers and climbers making their way up to the Gables, Scafell, Glaramara, and to the passes and pathways that lead over to Wasdale Head and Wastwater.

Just before the hamlet itself, on the western side of the valley, close by the tumbling Newhouse Gill, stand the remnants of the 'Borrowdale Yews' that inspired Wordsworth:

> "Those fraternal four of Borrowdale joined
> in one solemn and capacious grove"

Above these lie the spoil heaps of deserted plumbago mines. The pipes of graphite here, known as 'wadd' to the locals, were mined, on and off, depending on demand, for around three hundred years. Accurate dates of discovery and closure are elusive, but it seems likely that the 'wadd' was not actively mined until after 1577, and that these mines eventually closed around 1865. Initially used for medicinal purposes and marking sheep, it later became valued for dying cloth, for casting bomb shells, round shot and cannonballs, and as an element in glazing and hardening crucibles. Eventually, around the 1790s, it proved the basis for the once thriving Keswick pencil industry. The 'wadd' was relatively easy to steal, and the tales of pilfering by the miners, smuggling, and illegal trade are legion in the district. The evidence of the considerable security measures attempted by the mine owners in the buildings at the head of the mines, suggests that this was a major problem that had to be taken seriously.

During the periods of serious commercial mining, the houses at Seathwaite accommodated the miners, initially as batchelor residents, but later on in the nineteenth century, with their wives and children.

The magnet of the 'wadd' must have quadrupled the normal population of the tiny hamlet, and, difficult as it might be for us to imagine now, given it something of the bustle of an industrial settlement.

Severely exposed, the workings hang on the steep slopes near Newhouse Gill, and the miners would strike up the fell from their lodgings in Seathwaite to dig out the black gold, wash it, and load it on to pack horses that would pick their way down among the stony pathways of the valley to Keswick and beyond.

> Past these workings, as a young boy in *Rogue Herries*, his head full of stories about rascals who smuggled scraps of plumbago to sell to the Jews in Keswick, rode David Herries:
>
> "...today he was out to catch fish, and it was by the bridge under Stye Head that he would catch them - were he lucky!"

This would be Stockley Bridge, a major crossing point below the fells at the head of the Borrowdale valley.

The name 'Stockley', unusual in an area so prone to Scandinavian influence, derives from an Old

Stockley Bridge

English word meaning 'the place in the clearing' and appears as a place name in the thirteenth century records of the monks of Furness Abbey.

Everywhere near here resounds to the noise of running water, from the streams and the plethora of single and multiple waterfalls that drop off the sides of the fells. Dropping five hundred feet from the hanging valley near Sty Head path, the series of waterfalls known as Taylorgill Force is best viewed just before Stockley Bridge, and is particularly impressive after heavy rainfall.

David Herries moved to and fro, now above, then below the bridge, but the fish were not biting:

"He sat, his legs apart, his eyes intently fixed on the water. A shadow was flung. He looked up. Leaning on the bridge, looking down at him gravely was a pedlar with a coloured hat and a sharp bright face. 'You will be married' said the pedlar, 'and have fine sons'.
'How do you know?' asked David.
'I know everything' said the pedlar. 'I am the devil'.
David believed him. He looked wicked and gay as he stood there in the sunlight and Francis Herries had always told him that the devil was both these things".

Boys fishing and tinkers posing as the devil are rare in the present day movements around Stockley Bridge, although the occasional bather has been seen braving the chill waters of the gill. The main purpose of those who throw their shadow across the waters today are the famous

42

heights of the valley. The path from the bridge up to the Sty is one of the most popular walks in the northern fells and its substantial erosion bears testament to the thousands of feet that every year make their way over this ancient path to Wasdale.

It is from Wasdale that an older and bolder David Herries steals his bride. Following the Lingmell Beck, up between Lingmell and the 'Gavel' (Great Gable), David and Sarah are chased in thickening mist by a frantic uncle and his aid.

Over Sty Head, David braces himself and prepares to do battle with them:

> "Then he saw the rising ground that leads past Sprinkling Tarn and Allen Crags to Esk Hause. 'That would be better', and, with her following, he took the higher fell."

The pursuers eventually catch up with the fugitives near the dark tarn, and the shadowy figures wrestle nervously in the swirling mist. The struggle ends with David hurling the old man into the icy waters of Sprinkling Tarn:

> "The man splashed, sank, did not rise. Heaving with gusts of strangled breath, David waited. The ripples died under the moon but Denburn did not come up again. The scene was as a glass mirror and the quiet wonderful".

The word Tarn is thought to derive from an old Norse word meaning 'teardrop'; highly descriptive of the shape and scale of the small tarns relative to their great neighbours in the valleys below. Sty Head Tarn makes an ideal 'teardrop' below Great Gable, but Sprinkling Tarn, a little bit bigger, and tucked below Great End and Scafell Pike, is shaped more like a stone-age arrow head, pointing north out towards Seathwaite and away from some of the highest points in lakeland.

It still holds its dark secret. A favourite pause for walkers and climbers as they proceed to the more strenuous crags above Wasdale, a few will remember it as the site of old man Denburn's fate one foggy night in Hugh Walpole's imagination.

One of the most beautiful of the smaller tarns, its place in the wild scenery above Seathwaite can be appreciated from a variety of vantage points; particularly fine is the view of it from the northern edge of Great End, reserved for the more energetic, its rewards are quite spectacular. On the top of Great End you are in the midst of some of the grandest and most savage scenery in England. Strangely, not one of the most popular of the high peaks in the fells, the view to the north on a fine day is stunning, rising from Sprinkling Tarn below, over the bumps and lumps of the Seathwaite Fells, down Grains Gill into the Borrowdale Valley, and on to Derwentwater, Keswick and finally to Skiddaw and Blencathra far away on the northern skyline. The views in other directions are less dramatic but still give a strong sense of being at the centre of a rocky fortress. To the north-west is Great Gable and Kirk Fell, to the North-East Glaramara, to the South-East Esk Pike, Bowfell and Crinkle Crags, to the South-West Broad Crag and Scafell Pike.

Two of the most famous symbols of these high places are Scafell Pike and Great Gable. One the highest point in England (3,206 feet), the other the most famous haunt and nursery of rock climbers, since Haskett-Smith made the first ascent of Napes Needle, (a fantastic sixty foot spire of naked rock on its western front) in 1886.

Both have a special place on the 'roof of England'. From the area between these two peaks, the chiselling glaciers of the Pleistocene ice age moved out from their central dome to scrape and gouge the valleys around them, giving them the shape and contour that we see today.

Great Gable (or The Gavel), represents to many the real spirit of Lakeland. Rising up out of the northern end of Wasdale its western crags and screes host some of the most colourful climbs in the district. Great Hell Gate, Eagle's Nest Ridge, Little Hell Gate, all pretty meaningless to the average visitor, but the meat and drink of essential detail to the serious rock-man. The best views of its western face are those from Lingmell Crag or whilst taking the Corridor Route to the Scafells.

Often photographed from Wasdale Head for its solidity and Gable-end profile, it can also feature dramatically at the end of the valley, (mist obliging), in photographs taken from as far away as the western tip of Wastwater. On the

Borrowdale side, with its companion Green Gable it seems less interesting, just a couple of bald heads; but their lower slopes do touch Sty Head Pass, that great artery of the western falls, and guard over Sty Head Tarn, just a 'teardrop' below them.

Now a sort of monument, Great Gable was given to the National Trust in 1923 by the Fell and Rock Climbing Club in memory of its members who died in the First World War. A bronze tablet with a memorial inscription and a reief showing some of the neighbouring peaks has been placed on a boulder near the summit cairn. However, the most dramatic view of Wasdale and Wastwater is not from the summit itself but from the Westmoreland Cairn just below it.

Scafell and Scafell Pike have been a magnet for the serious, and the casual climber for nearly 200 years. Probably the most celebrated casual ascent of Scafell, certainly the first to be recorded, was that by Samuel Taylor Coleridge on 5 August 1802. He climbed up from Wasdale Head by way of the old 'corpse road' to Burnmoor Tarn and then took the long slog up Green How; after a succession of resting, walking, resting, climbing and resting sessions that seem quite understandable to the present writer he stood on the top:

> " ... believed by the Shepherds here to be higher than either Helvellyn or Skiddaw ... "

Then gazing into Mickledore, and desperate to get up onto Scafell Pike, (which his map told him was Bow Fell), and:

> " ... too confident and too indolent to look around and wind till I find a track or other symptom of safety ... "

he scrambled down the precipitous ledges and slabs above the col, probably by way of Scafell Chimney, and reached Mickledore, his legs all a-tremble and his chest covered in 'great red heat lumps'.

Later the more cautious Wordsworth, complete with 'shepherd guide' climbed up to Scafell Pike from Esk Hause and included a note on the wonder of the scene that greeted him in his highly profitable 'Guide to the Lakes', which was published in 1810.

> "The stillness seemed to be not of this world: we paused, and kept silence to listen; and no sound could be heard: the Scawfell Cataracts were voiceless to us: and there was not an insect hum in the air ... But the majesty of the mountains below, and close to us, is not to be conceived. We now beheld the whole mass of Great Gavel from its base – the Den of Wastdale at our feet – a gulf immeasurable."

Many thousands have tasted that stillness since, so much so that the popular footpaths around the Lords Rake and the West Wall Traverse, are now so dangerously eroded that they require extra special care if used as an approach to the summit.

There is little hint of precaution or preparation in Walpole's *Vanessa,* when one changeable November day in 1928 Tom and Sally Herries, children of different mothers, but one father, and re-acquainted after some years apart, set out on a grand expedition. Entirely in tune with the spirit of Coleridge they would go " ... up Stye Head, climb Scafell and be back for supper":

> "They crossed the little Stockley Bridge. They had been hemmed in by Glaramara on the left and Base Brown on the right, and now the sharp precipices of Great End filled up the valley in front. It was here that Sally had the first perception that she was moving into an uncertain world. They reached Stye Head Tarn ... it was very cold, but they found shelter behind a rock on the slope of Green Gable, looked down to the Tarn across the flat, and ate their luncheon. This was the very wildest scenery that Sally had ever beheld".

Tom recalls how David Herries fought his momentous duel at Sprinkling Tarn just above Sty Head, then looking down into the autumn greens of Eskdale as they go, they walk up the slope to Esk Hause and, as many walkers do today, started to climb slowly up the track to Scafell Pike:

> " ... Then a moment later, from no quarter at all as it seemed, a blinding storm came upon

Sty Head Tarn, Great End and the Scafell Range

them. There was snow in it and a wet mist, and it appeared to Tom that from below them, on either side, a boiling vapour of mist rushed, edging up".

Suddenly in driving sleet the familiar becomes unkown and they stumble together on the 'Pike' seeking shelter from the blast. Tom manages to cram Sally into the safety of an arched rock, while he, trying to stay awake, moves about on the mountain.

"He ran foward and fell."

Tom's fictional death in *Vanessa* has all too often been mirrored in reality. After Helvellyn, the Scafells attract more walkers than any other fell in the Lake District, and thus by virtue of sheer numbers, its accident rate is high, including many fatalities. Some of the early climbers who died here are buried in the tiny churchyard at Wasdale Head.

Weather is the great enemy; extremes of cold, snow and swiftly descending mists are common on the tops, and despite the attractions of light clothing, especially in summer, proper footwear, waterprooofs and an early start are essential ingredients for a safe trip up to the 'Pike'.

How to get there

There are many, many different approaches to some of the features that I have mentioned in this section. I have chosen two walks which are personal favourites of mine and which I feel provide some spectacular viewpoints for the walker and photographer.

1. The Grains Gill route to Great End, Scafell Pike and Sprinkling Tarn, returning by the Sty Head track.

This particular walk has the virtue of providing one or two clear options at particular points, to cut short the walk and return by way of Sty Head if the weather, tiredness or both, should suggest a shorter excursion.

Maps

Outdoor Leisure Maps O.S. 1:25,000 NW and SW sheets and O.S. 1:50,000 (pink covers) sheet 90 Penrith and Keswick.

By Bus

Take the Keswick-Seatoller No. 79 service, (see times at Keswick, Grange or Seatoller). Alight at Seatoller and walk for fifty yards towards Rosthwaite turning right into the road signposted Seathwaite. The road follows the river and the western wall of the valley offering impressive views of the high fells to the south. An undiscovered land as far as most motorised photographers are concerned; under the right conditions the mile long walk along this road offers considerable scope for some interesting picture-taking.

By Car

Take the B5289 from Keswick, past Derwentwater, Grange, through Rosthwaite for just over a mile turning off left to Seathwaite. Park your car on the left-hand side of the road just before the buildings. An early arrival is suggested as this must be one of the most popular car parks in the Lake District.

The sometimes roaring waterfall dropping steeply off the fellside opposite the parking area is Sourmilk Gill.

The Walk starting from Seathwaite

Walk through miniscule Seathwaite, forebearing at the moment to test the fresh trout that is on sale here during the season, but noting the small cafe on your left, (this could be a godsend on your way back), and take the wide, stony pathway due south away from the houses.

The steep slopes of Glaramara go up on your left while the sprawling Base Brown rises off to your right. If you are lucky you will be able to hear and then see the mighty Taylor Gill Force which tumbles down the southern side of Base Brown.

There are many fine pictures to be taken along this path using both wide-angle lenses to take in the full power and force of the fells at the head of the valley, and medium telephoto lenses to pick out waterfalls, pathways and other bits of interesting detail.

When looking for interesting compositions here, try moving up on to some of the grassy banks to the left of the track or off to the right on some of the boulders near the stream. If you have good waterproof boots on, try a spot in the middle of the stream looking up past Stockley Bridge to the fells above it.

At the bridge itself pause to enjoy the situation of this famous pack-horse crossing, one of the most famous junctions in Lakeland. Here the pathway separates, one branch at right-angles to the bridge, goes up to Sty Head, the other less popular route follows Grains Gill between Glaramara and Seathwaite Fell.

Take the Grains Gill path; it is quite easy at first, becoming gradually steeper later on after crossing the stream. The contours now become closer and this is the time for more frequent stops, to rest, to look back, and to take some photographs. The twin peaks of Skiddaw grow and grow as you move up the steeper part of the path, as does little Castle Crag in Borrowdale, and Derwentwater itself beyond it. On your right as you look back the ragged peaks of Glaramara become clearer, their sides cut through with gullies and ravines.

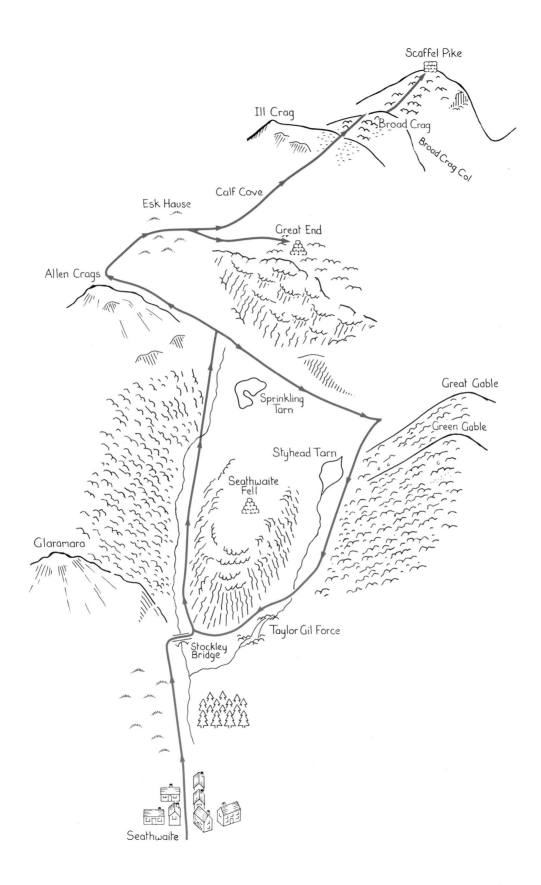

Scaffel Pike

Ill Crag

Broad Crag

Broad Crag Col

Calf Cove

Esk Hause

Great End

Allen Crags

Great Gable

Green Gable

Sprinkling
Tarn

Styhead Tarn

Seathwaite
Fell

Glaramara

Taylor Gil Force

Stockley
Bridge

Seathwaite

Great End from Esk Hause

In front the massive face of Great End catches the morning light high above the dark ravine which now carries the gill down below the path. Keep this ravine on your right as you move up past the 2,000 feet mark to cross the little ford at the junction with the famous Eskdale-Wasdale route that now crosses directly in front of you.

To the right this path goes down to Sprinkling Tarn, an ideal diversion for a picnic, or to cut short your walk by proceeding over Sty Head and back to Seathwaite. For those still stout of heart and foot, the route onwards and upwards is the left-hand path which eventually turns off to the right up to the grassy plateau of Esk Hause.

From here take in the splendid form of Esk Pike, 2,903 feet high (1885 metres) with the clear path to its summit going off up on your left. Just away behind it is the interesting Pike O'Stickle with the

Great Gable from the path to Scafell Pike

square looking summit of Harrison Stickle just beyond that. There is time to explore the possibility of some pictures here, possibly using a telephoto lens to pull in some of the detail of the surrounding peaks.

After taking in the various viewpoints here take the path to the right that swings around the back of Great End. Here at Calf Cove another possibility offers itself, by taking off to the right you can cut short your journey and ascend the rocky slopes of Great End, 2,984 feet (910 metres) and some of the finest views in the area.

For those determined on Scafell Pike, brace yourself for the long slog up the slopes of Ill Crag, down into the col, up the rocky slope to Broad Crag, skirting the summit itself, and then down again into another col.

"Path" is too good a name for much of this route; there are plenty of cairns but no real path or track. You will have to hop from boulder to boulder using the cairns as signposts, and encouraged by the occasional sight of the square cairn on Scafell Pike. Look out for pictures though, particularly to the N.W. for fine views of Great Gable and Kirk Fell.

The route now rises out of the col quite steeply, still among the boulders, but with more of a path, up to the top of Scafell Pike. You have made it, the highest point in England, 3,210 feet, (978 metres), jump up on the cairn and celebrate. Unfortunately, the summit is not terribly impressive as summits go, a wild and wasteful place covered with the ubiquitous boulders.

To make the most of your camera, you will need to wander about the summit looking for the best

49

pictures in each direction. Part of Wastwater can be seen, Sea Fell itself, the summit of Lingmell well below, and the craggy south face of Great Gable. Watch what the light is doing, what shadows the clouds are making, where the people are, (this is the M1 of walking routes), and what they are wearing, a brightly clad fellow walker might give some useful scale to a wide shot of the surrounding peaks.

The route back is the same until you come to the top of Grains Gill, here keep on the path below Great End, past Sprinkling Tarn and down to Sty Head. If there is still enough light look out for interesting detail on Great Gable, for reflections in both the tarns and for possible evening light on Borrowdale from near the top of Grains Gill.

The Sty Head pass track back down to Seathwaite is easy to follow, although it gets caught up in the Sty Head Gill at times. It is being restored by the National Trust and the Manpower Services Commission and the lower, steeper end has been distinctly improved by their attention. The path soon drops down towards Stockley Bridge and the stony path back to Seathwaite, signalling the end of a ten mile round trip, which, if the weather has been kind, should have offered the prospect of some fine photography.

2. To Great Gable from the top of the Honister Pass

Maps

Outdoor Leisure Map O.S. 1:25,000 S.W. Sheet and O.S. 1:50,000 (pink covers) Sheet 89 West Cumbria.

By Bus

To Seatoller, then a 1½ mile walk up to the pass using the tarmac road or the grassy pathways that, nearer the top, run alongside it.

By Car

Drive along the B5289 to the car park down behind the Youth Hostel at the top of the Honister Pass. This can be approached from both the Buttermere and the Keswick side via steep gradients and low gears.

The Walk

One comforting thought as you begin this walk through the gate at the southern end of the Youth Hostel car park is that starting off at nearly 1,200 feet there is only 1,759 to go to the summit of Great Gable, height 2,949 feet (899 metres).

The route, which is quite steep at first, goes straight up the fence from the car park to the summit of Grey Knotts. The path is clearly shown on the map, and enough feet have been over this grassy/rocky slope to show the way. Stick near to the fence at the start just above the quarry and move away from the steeper bits near it as and when it suits you.

As you ascend here, take some time out to look for pictures over the slate quarry, (during a weekday you will not escape the sound of the quarry digger until you are well over Brandreth), the Honister Pass itself, Honister Crag and the path directly opposite going up to Dale Head. Over to the east is Borrowdale, the Watendlath fells and the great Helvellyn range.

The summit of Grey Knotts is interesting; it ranges over quite a large area and provides some lovely views of Buttermere and Crummock Water to the west. The path to Brandreth is quite clear, but I would recommend wandering about as you move down from Grey Knotts. Look out for the wrinkled top of Haystacks, and the fine profile of Pillar, especially when it has a sprinkling of snow on it. Be prepared to change lenses here taking opportunities for both wide angle and telephoto compositions.

The summit of Brandreth itself is dull, but it does offer some interesting views on the eastern side over towards Seathwaite and Glaramara, and to Ennerdale in the west.

These views continue on the walk up the gentle slope to Green Gable, opening up access to such details as the Sty Head and Sprinkling Tarns, and the massive arc of Gable Crag as you pass over the summit.

Take care as you descend from Green Gable, the red coloured path to Windy Gap is rocky, and

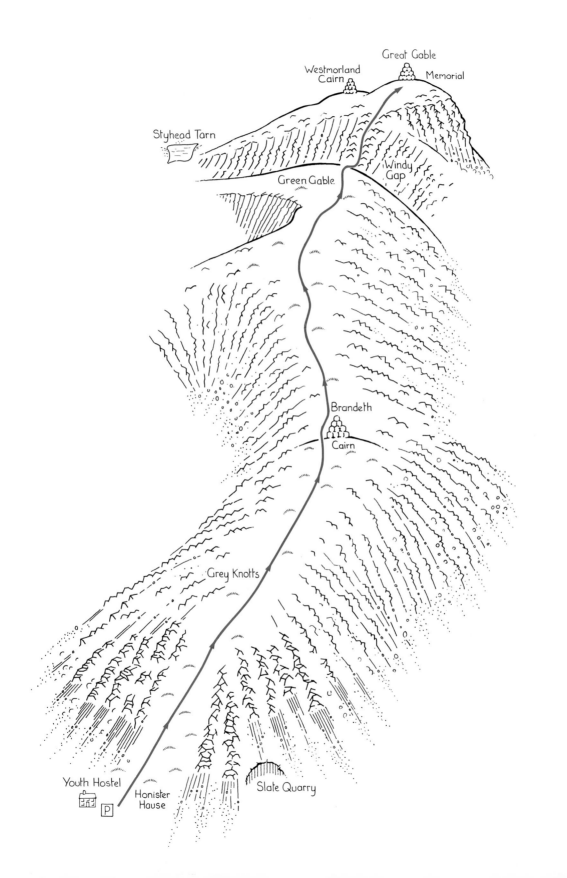

Great Gable

Westmorland
Cairn

Memorial

Styhead Tarn

Windy
Gap

Green Gable

Brandeth

Cairn

Grey Knotts

Youth Hostel

Honister
Hause

Slate Quarry

Summit memorial on Great Gable

some of it is quite loose. At Windy Gap you now face a bit of a slog up to Great Gable itself, not a terribly good path, rocky and a bit steep to start with but becoming easier after a short while providing a gentler, if still rocky walk up to the top.

This really is a summit, an exhilarating place. You feel that you have made it to the top of a real mountain. Examine the war memorial and its relief map of the surrounding fells and then move off the top for a few yards towards the Wasdale side of the summit to the Westmorland Cairn.

Here on a clear day you get a truly magnificent view of Wasdale Head with its famous network of stone walls and the mysterious Wastwater directly behind it.

This is a place for a camera, try a variety of focal lengths. Detail from the great Scafell range can be picked out from here with a telephoto lens, and the great panorama of Wasdale Head cries out for a wide angle approach.

Again make time to explore the top, testing the views with different lenses and filters, making the most of your time on this, one of the most attractive viewpoints in the Lakes.

My own preference is to return by the same route. I think that the path is slightly easier to return by, and the extraordinary views can now be taken in with a slightly different emphasis as you return northwards.

A popular alternative is to take the path off the summit to Beck Head, winding away by Stony Cove below Gable Crag to catch up with the Moses Trod path, skirting the slopes of Brandreth and Grey Knotts, eventually joining the dismantled tramway route down to the Slate works and the road.

Personally I find this a tedious route to return by, and if you are inclined to try it I would recommend using it on the outward journey for the views to the west and north-west, returning over the tops via Green Gable, Brandreth and Grey Knotts.

The Helvellyn range from the slopes of Grey Knotts above Honister

Grange village from the Borrowdale road

Grange-in-Borrowdale Derwent Farm, and the Lodore Falls

Once a storehouse and farm for the monks of Furness Abbey, the small village of Grange-in-Borrowdale stands at the northern head of the Borrowdale valley, a huddle of grey stone houses at the side of the intriguing double-arched bridge over the River Derwent. The bridge was built in 1675, and some of the houses in the village, like Fell View, were constructed from stone taken from the old monks granary. The road over the bridge leads to the western side of Derwentwater, towards Manesty, Walpole's Brackenburn and Brandelow Park. As it winds away from Grange it offers superb views of the crags and woods on the lake's eastern shore, and just below it lies Brandelhow Bay, a particularly beautiful corner of the lake on its western side, and one that Walpole would have enjoyed many times, in all its seasons, lying as it does so close to Brackenburn.

Grange has a special place in the gestation of the Herries novels, a frequent crossroads in the stories, it was also a favourite social and business haunt for Walpole himself. His nearest village, he knew the buildings and the people in them well, he walked and drove through it often and was fascinated by its position as the gateway to his favourite valley.

South of the village the valley narrows to the Jaws of Borrowdale where Castle Crag stands like a sentinel, and the rocks on the eastern side of the road seem to press their shoulders forward, squeezing the River Derwent into its narrow passageway. Walpole's house at Brackenburn was built with stone quarried from "Dalt Wood" just south of Grange and a pathway from the village to Seatoller, at the head of Honister, passes these, and other workings, as it threads below the western flank of the Borrowdale valley. From this path it is possible to see Hollows Farm which lies below a classic geological site, being the point where the smooth Skiddaw Slate of Maiden Moor meets the craggy Borrowdale Volcanics of High Spy.

It was to Grange one 'overhanging autumn day' in *Rogue Herries*, that old Mrs Wilson, a member of the Herries household long suspected of being a witch, came through the woods and copses on the eastern bank of the river, to visit the sick bed of her childhood friend Hannah Mounsey:

> "The old woman moved on. She paused before she crossed the bridge that raised itself up like a cat's back over the divided strands of the river."
> "She knew Hannah's cottage, a little grey dwelling twisted like a crumpled ear over the river."

She had arrived too late, Hannah was dead, the house was dark and still and Hannah's dumbfounded husband sat still and mute in his bright red nightcap.

Outside the house a crowd of villagers gather, silently waiting for her to come out of the cottage. As she does, they set on her and violently drag her to the river, chanting and shouting as one of them carries her up to the top of the bridge:

> "He lifted his stout arms and flung her out, high into the air. The little white body gleamed for a moment, then fell like a stone, into the water."

The hysteria is cut short by the dramatic arrival of Rogue Herries, who plunges into the river to retrieve her body and bring it to the bank before the eyes of the now silent mob.

These days the divers who leap from the bridge in summer, a precarious adventure to the casual bystander, hardly give old Mrs Wilson and her spells a second thought. For them sinking into the River Derwent is a temporary rather than a terminal experience.

Walpole was a frequent visitor to George Mounsey at the Manor House in Grange, just down the road from Brackenburn. George and his brother John carried out a number of building and decorating jobs for Walpole at Brackenburn during the 1930s, and he would have been familiar with the house attached to George Mounsey's, the Derwent Farm.

This is a typical seventeenth century Lakeland house, with its 'House', 'Hallan', 'Down House' and 'Hooded Hearth' and it is quite possibly the model for Statesman Peel's house in *Rogue Herries*.

At this fictional house set somewhere in the meadows along the River Derwent, not far from the bridge at Grange, Rogue Herries and his children attend a wild party on Christmas night 1737.

J D Marshall in his 'Old Lakeland', 1971, however, argues that Walpole's description of the house is misleading, as few members of the yeoman class had rooms large enough to accommodate the sort of Christmas gathering that Walpole depicted. Accurate or not, Peel's party is an eventful affair. Here Francis Herries meets the eight-year-old child Mirabell Starr, and her mother Jane Starr, to whom he had once given his coat below the Lodore Falls. Here also he fought a duel, in a frosty field behind Peel's house, with young Osbaldistone from Threapthwaite, and was badly slashed on his cheek.

The participants are at large before a broad canvas, and Walpole uses the opportunity to give full rein to his formidable descriptive powers. He is at his best as the festivities begin to degenerate:

> "The Christmas feast was at its height. This was a scene from Breughel . . . An old man with long white hair, thin as a scarecrow, was dancing very solemnly alone in the middle of the floor, twisting his body into corkscrew shapes . . . But wildness was coming in, coming in from the caverns of the hill, and the high cold spaces round Sprinkling Tarn and the lonely passes above the listening valleys. It was Christ's day no longer. He had been turned out when the wind changed, and all the doors and shutters of the house had rattled their shoulders at His going."

Unlike some Herries locations we can only picture this scene in our mind's eye, because, as Walpole says:

Grange Farm

"There is no house like Peel's house anywhere in England anymore . . ."

We have to imagine that it was here, somewhere, close to the Derwent and closed in by the valley of Borrowdale.

Not far from Grange, towards Keswick, below Gowder and Shepherds Crag, near the southern tip of Derwentwater, stand the Lodore Falls. Fed by the rains that fall on the Watendlath Fells and High Seat just above them, they pour grandly over mighty boulders, hemmed in by high wooded cliffs.

57

Many famous visitors have clambered up through the woods to stand below the falls and many of them have left us a record of their impressions. Thomas Gray, a pioneering tourist recorded his visit to Lodore in his 'Journal' in 1769:

"... the height appeared to be about 200 feet, the quantity of water not great, though (these three days excepted) it had rained daily in the hills for near two months before; but then the stream was nobly broken, leaping from rock to rock, and foaming with fury. On one side a towering Crag, that spired up to equal if not overtop the neighbouring cliffs (this lay all in shade and darkness); on the other hand a rounder, broader, projecting hill shagged with wood, and illuminated by the sun which glanced sideways on the upper part of the cataract."

Ten years later the twenty year old William Wilberforce, later to labour so effectively against the slave trade, while agreeing with Gray on the variable power of the torrent, is much more effusive about their setting; his diary entry for the day notes that:

"Considered as a Waterfall I have seen superior, but taking in the accompaniments, the immense Rock on the left steep as a Castle Wall and whiter than they generally are in this country, seen sometimes bare, sometimes through Trees fantastically disposed, with the back view of the Lake, never could such a scene enter in the Imagination of Man to conceive. The fall is not a perpendicular one but the Rocks and Stones which prevent it being so it has by its own Violence strewed the way with, and it leaps over them with irresistible fury ..."

A temperamental cascade, Lodore can be a spectacular torrent after heavy rain, and a miserable disappointment in high summer, or after a lengthy dry spell, in this it is as unpredictable now as it was for those early reporters.

Walking near the boulders in the wood below the falls, one September morning in *Rogue Herries,* Francis Herries gave his fine plum-coloured coat laced with silver, to a shivering woman beside a dead man with his throat cut:

"Out on the Watendlath path, looking up at a bright silver waterfall poised like a broken ladder against the green cliff, he had seen by the stones of the beck a dead man with his throat cut and a woman shivering beside him. A dead man was no extraordinary sight; this man was naked save for his shirt, and his white legs stretched stiffly as though they had been carved. The woman did not cry, or ask for alms, but she shivered in the keen September air. He did not speak to her, but obeying the impulse of the instant, took off his plum-coloured coat and threw it over her trembling shoulders.
He strode back to the house."

Within a few minutes both the woman and the body had disappeared into the mystery of the wood, and the bright green mosses of Lodore lay still again.

Lodore Wood

How to get there

Maps

Outdoor Leisure Map O.S. 1:25,000 N.W. sheet, O.S. 1:50,000 (pink covers) sheet 89 West Cumbria or sheet 90 Penrith and Keswick.

By Bus

Using service No. 79 the Keswick to Seatoller service alighting at Grange-in-Borrowdale.

By Car

Along the B5289 south from Keswick to Grange-in-Borrowdale parking in the small car park by the bridge or at some other suitable place off the road.

The Walk

Grange and the Lodore Falls

Walk up through the village of Grange, perhaps stopping to have a peep in the litte church, and to note the views of Skiddaw across the meadows that run away from the church down to Derwentwater. Bear right on the road past the Borrowdale Gates Hotel, looking back to take in the village rooftops and the steep cliffs of Grange Crags rising above them.

Follow the road up past the Borrowdale Gates Hotel until you come near to the Manesty woods off on your right. Take the wide track on your left up the south-eastern slopes of Cat Bells. After a

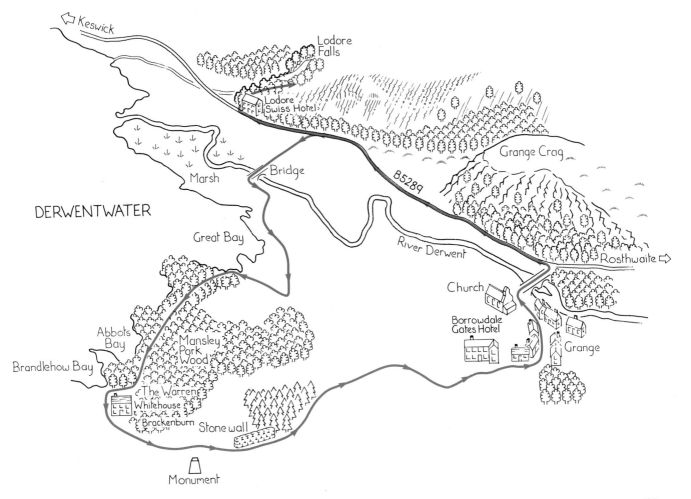

short time look out for the narrower shale-covered path that leads off to the right through some bracken and alongside a dry-stone wall, this eventually broadens out and brings you to the slate seat and commemorative plaque erected by Harold Cheevers in memory of Hugh Walpole. This was one of Walpole's favourite viewpoints and stands just above Brackenburn where he lived and where he wrote much of the *Herries Chronicle*.

After taking in the fine panorama, drop down the steep path just to the left of the seat that comes out on the road at the side of Brackenburn.

From this lakeside roadway, which I think offers one of the finest and most accessible views across Derwentwater. A number of interesting walks are possible, including one that starts a little way down the road through the lovely Brandelhow woods to lakeside paths that wind through Brandelhow Park northwards to Hawes End.

To continue the walk to Lodore take the clear stony pathway almost opposite the side of Brackenburn down to Brandelhow Bay and the (private) boathouses. After taking in the lakeside views here continue along the path off to your right alongside the white pebbledashed house signed 'Brandlehow' up through a gate to the wood beyond, past the low stone bungalow signed 'The Warren', and onto the path signposted 'Footpath to Lodore' which goes off on your left.

The little bays and coves here are all well worth exploring, giving some lovely views over the lake to the north and north-east towards Blencathra and Walla Crag. Carry on through the wood, over the simple log bridges that cross the many streams here, skirting the edge of the lake towards a dry-stone wall, through the wooden gate moving away from the lakeside and rising up a little way to some marshy ground that now offers a fine prospect southwards to Castle Crag, the Jaws of Borrowdale and the solid wall of Great End rising up at the head of the valley.

Carry on to the concrete bridge on stone piers that crosses the River Derwent here just before it enters the lake. As you cross the bridge look out for

Brandelhow Bay, Derwentwater near Brackenburn

The Jaws of Borrowdale

rock climbers directly in front of you, testing the smooth rock on the lower slopes of Shepherds Crag. From the bridge follow the wide, (sometimes flooded) path to the Borrowdale road. Turn left onto the road and look out for the entrance on your right that leads around the back of the Lodore Swiss Hotel. Go up the drive noting the honesty (5p) box set into the back wall of the hotel, (do they save it all up for a party?), through the gate, across the wooden bridge and up into the rocky wood to hear and see, with a bit of luck, the 'smashing and crashing' of the famous Lodore Falls. This is a fascinating place after heavy rain, ideal for some interesting photographs of water, trees and moss-covered rocks. Hand-held photography is possible, although it can be quite dark in among the trees and against the steep rocks that rise up at the back of the falls. Some fast film might be a good investment for serious picture-taking here and a tripod is a must if you want to experiment with some slow shutter speeds to turn the waters of the Watendlath beck into soft milky streaks as it tumbles over the rocks

There is a pleasant path northwards through the Lodore Wood which comes out on the road again opposite a lakeside car park. On a bright day after a night of rain the green mosses here give out a magical luminescence in the tree-filtered sunlight which is quite remarkable and a great challenge to the energetic photographer.

Return from this path, or from the path behind the hotel and take the Borrowdale road back to Grange, perhaps enjoying a pause on the bridge before catching your bus or returning to your car

The Lodore Falls

Honister,
Buttermere and the
Vale of Newlands

Honister Crag towers menacingly over the Honister Pass that links Buttermere with Borrowdale. Leading up and on to Fleetwith Pike, its steep cliffs are deservedly called 'crag', and deny all but the most experienced climbers access from Honister Pass itself. However, an exciting path to the top of the Crag can be taken from Gatesgarth Cottage at the Buttermere end of the pass, or from Honister Hause on the Borrowdale side.

In *Rogue Herries*, Francis falls asleep in the pass and on waking is taken by a thin-faced vagabond to a cave at the back of Honister Crag:

> "They struck up the fell to the left and climbed. The man led the horse patiently and with kindness. When they were high on the moor they could see the guards of the mines pacing on the path below ... On the brow of the hill the man took Herries' arm, led him over boulders, dipped down the shelving turf, then pushed up again on the hinder shoulder of Honister ... He could see icily blue, the thin end of Buttermere Lake far below."

The stranger leads Francis to the grey opening of a cave in the hill, half hidden by bracken and furze.

Inside the cave he found the fascinating sixteen year old girl, Mirabell Starr, whom he had met as a child with her mother at the Christmas party at Statesman Peel's house:

> "In the black cavern beyond him there was a fire, and on the fire a round black pot. A girl sat on the ground watching the pot. At once he knew her."

He had found the girl again, high on the wind-blown crags above Honister, the flame haired

Honister Crag towering above the Honister Pass

The Honister Pass

daughter of the trembling woman he had met below the Lodore Falls.

Today we are unlikely to find a gypsy girl in a cave, but the views over Fleetwith Pike and Haystacks, down to Buttermere, and across to Robinson and Hindscarth well repay the walk up the path to Honister Crag.

In the fourth Herries novel, *Vanessa*, Walpole causes the restless Benjie to want to walk from Cold Fell house in the Vale of Newlands over Hindscarth and Robinson down to Buttermere and then over Red Pike into Ennerdale. Well pregnant, Vanessa feels that she must accompany him, despite the signs of an impending storm. They step it out together, up the valley sides towards Dale Head, past the old Goldscope workings, just as many walkers do today.

In a single day on the high fells in Cumbria walkers, and photographers, can experience dramatically different climatic conditions. Bright sunshine, heavy black cloud, rain, hail, clear blue skies; running out of one into another just by crossing over into the next valley.

Thus it was for Benjie and Vanessa. As they reach the high places at the end of the valley the weather deteriorates rapidly but, undeterred they press on, Benjie in his element, revelling in the storm, Vanessa suddenly gripped by the pain of impending childbirth. The storm broke:

> "Benjie knew the dangers of this piece of country. Robinson and Hindscarth had rough faces with much scree, and the ghylls into Buttermere had loose and falling rock with water suddenly, and sodden turf on the fell-side. A nasty ground for mist."

And then the rain:

> "It was as though a spirit with inky hair strode the fell and passed, blowing a great horn summoning his army! They could see the rain sweeping from the farthest horizon in curtains of gauze, blowing, bending, but never breaking."

Luckily, the two lovers come upon a white farmhouse, 'Randle Farm', near some trees by the side of a small beck. This haven could well have been by the trees near Kirk Close, and the beck could have been the Hassneshow Beck which runs beside them off Goat Crag near the path from Robinson to Buttermere. This is of course pure conjecture, Walpole does not make it clear and he could have meant anywhere below the fells here. However, the lovely walk from Newlands over Dale Head, Hindscarth Edge, and Robinson does lead naturally past these features and I think it a reasonable assumption that Vanessa's baby, Sally Herries, carying on the dual Herries tradition of illegitimacy and a storm-racked birthday, was born somewhere below Robinson near the side of Buttermere.

Walpole rarely uses the landscape around Buttermere in the Herries saga, yet it shares with Derwentwater and Wastwater a truly craggy and romantic landscape, with many famous fells, High Stile, Fleetwith Pike, Haystacks, Robinson and Goat Crag, standing guard above it.

For the motorist the most dramatic approach to this small lake is that from Keswick and Rosthwaite through the Honister Pass. Today the traveller who would make the most of this wild passage through the fells will have to rise early, or visit it well out of season to avoid bumper-to-bumper viewing. Along this route came early tourists in horse-drawn brakes doing the 'Buttermere Round', Keswick, Borrowdale, Honister, Buttermere, Newlands, Portinscale, and back to Keswick again. So steep were some of the

Robinson and Buttermere

ascents for the poor horses that the passengers had to complete certain sections on foot, and when they got back in again a special braking mechanism, called a 'slipper' had to be used to hold them back on some of the descents. No doubt the visitors refreshed all the parts they needed to reach at the Fish Inn, the celebrated home of Mary Robinson, the 'Beauty of Buttermere'. In 1802 she fell prey to John Hatfield, the notorious imposter, bigamist and forger. Posing as the Honourable Alexander Angustus Hope, he added Mary to his clutch of wives, honeymooned her around Cumbria and was eventually hanged, after a chat with Wordsworth, at Carlisle for franking his own letters.

The story of 'wronged' and 'spoiled' Mary was celebrated in chap-books and verse, and was even portrayed in melodramas on the London stage. Her parents quite unashamedly made the most of her fame, and business at the 'Fish' picked-up considerably. Quieter days awaited Mary though, she eventually married Richard Harrison, a Caldbeck farmer, bore him seven children, and spent the rest of her days in domestic obscurity. She died aged 58 and was buried in Caldbeck churchyard, seventeen years before the famous huntsman John Peel went to earth there.

Nicholas Size, a later host at the Fish Inn also fancied his chances as an author, and with some success. In one of his novels, 'The Secret Valley', published in 1930, (the same year as Rogue Herries), he describes a great battle when a vast Norman army from Cockermouth was brutally defeated by the native English, who descended on them from the fells above Rannerdale near Crummock Water. Hugh Walpole unselfishly gave advice and encouragement to the landlord author, as he did to many struggling and aspiring writers.

Nicholas Size outlived his mentor, he was still at the Fish Inn in the 1950s, and when he died he was buried overlooking his 'Secret Valley', a romantic statement about the fells which Hugh Walpole would no doubt have approved of.

To the north-west of Buttermere village lie a range of fells and crags that drop down from Robinson and Hindscarth into the gentle Vale of Newlands.

Walpole chose this valley as the place in *Vanessa* where Benjie and Vanessa live together at Cold Fell House after his return from the Boer War. Vanessa's mad husband still lives in London and they are exiled by the weight of their own and previous Herries scandals:

> "Cold Fell had changed not at all in the last hundred years, with its whitewashed front, its narrow passages and low-ceilinged rooms, the rough cobbling before the door, the slope down the hill where the hens were and the broad fields that crossed the stream and the valley . . ."

Cold Fell House may be here somewhere, perhaps disguised with another name. We get one or two clues. One day when Vanessa is sitting with Sally ". . . on the slope of the hill behind the white farm", she is able to see that ". . . a trap had drawn up at the gate behind the church . . ." Such a viewpoint might well coincide with the location of High Snab Farm, which is the present author's preference, then again perhaps it rests on the slopes near here only in Walpole's imagination. Either way, there is no disputing the beauty of this place.

Walpole also made good use of the very tangible Newlands Church. Benjie's tendency to disappear for two or three days at a time causes Vanessa many moments of despair:

> "Then she burst out of the house again and walked swiftly away from the hills . . . She came to the little church and, scarcely knowing that she did so, finding the door opened, entered.
> She had often, in the last six months, visited this little place and had grown to love it. Behind its wall, guarded by its trees, hills mounting to every side of it and one of the loveliest small rivers in England at its back, quiet, restrained and confident, it held something in its heart greater than change or fashion."

Rebuilt in 1843 the church lies at the fork of the valley, half way up its length, and stands today, with its little one room school at its side just as Walpole describes it.

The schoolroom, built by the parishioners in

A shepherd with a sick lamb outside Newlands Church

1877, was closed down as a school ninety years later in 1967. It has recently been restored and no doubt will be put to good use.

Truly, one of the most beautiful lowland locations used in the Herries novels; view the church and valley on a warm day in early spring and you are not surprised that Walpole uses this place as a quiet haven for Vanessa:

> "She heard a bird singing, the water swinging by, and the voice of a shepherd as he crossed the grass by the church wall . . ."

On the Keswick side of the road, branching off from the church, is Emerald Bank, once the home of Robert Southey's sailor brother Tom, the brother to whom he wrote in 1809, 'Tell the people how the water comes down at Lodore', sowing the seed for his 'shaking and quaking, pouring and roaring' poem thirteen years later.

Above the little church on the slopes below Maiden Moor lie the remains of one of the most famous mines in the Keswick area, the Goldscope Mines. Worked by the German miners of the Society for the Mines Royal from 1561 onwards they shipped lead and copper ores to the smelting works at Brigham on the River Greta, just to the east of Keswick. The copper vein here was reportedly nine feet thick, and exceptionally rich in workable ore. One of the lead veins was said to be fourteen feet thick, and this dual copper/lead facility ensured a lively, now open/now closed, policy by various mining interests right up until the years of the First World War.

The name 'Goldscope' is thought to be derived from the German 'Gottesgab' meaning 'God's Gift'; on the western side of Derwentwater another name, 'Copperheap Bay', still survives for the place on the shore where the ore was shipped across the lake for smelting.

Seen today it is difficult for us to envisage this tranquil valley as the setting for a vigorous industry, easier perhaps to imagine it as the hidden scene of Vanessa's desperate and illicit affair with the reckless Benjie.

How to get there

There are so many walks to be enjoyed around Honister, Buttermere and Newlands, including a very enjoyable walk around Buttermere itself which can be identified very easily by a close look at the map, that I have only been able to include two here:-

1. Fleetwith Pike from Gatesgarth
2. Dale Head from Honister Hause.

Map

For both walks, Outdoor Leisure Map O.S. 1:25,000 N.W. sheet Ennerdale and Derwent.

Fleetwith Pike - 2,126ft (648 metres)

By Bus

Use the Mountain Goat minibus service that runs between Keswick, via Newlands to the Fish Inn at Buttermere, then walking the 1¾ miles or so along the road to Gatesgarth, enjoying the fine views of all the main fells around Buttermere en route.

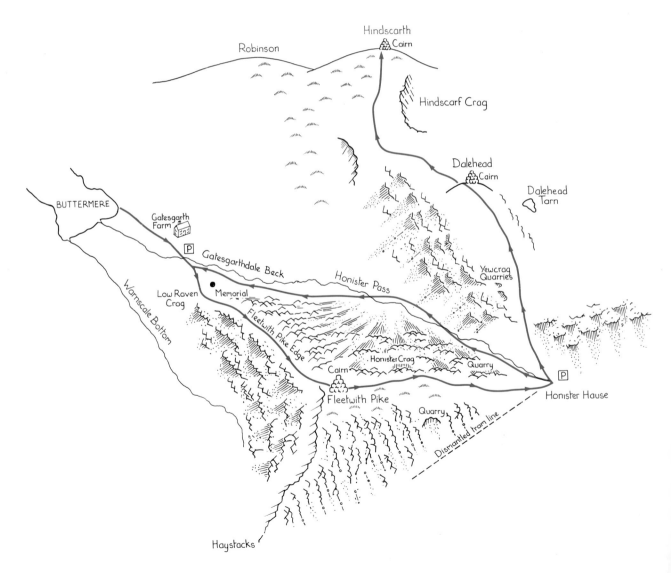

By Car

From Keswick two delightful routes are available, the one taking the B5289 Borrowdale road south along the eastern edge of Derwentwater through Borrowdale, past Seatoller and up the steep climb to Honister Hause, dropping down into the Honister Pass itself to park at Gatesgarth. This must be one of the most thrilling drives in the Lake District including as it does so many different and interesting features in under twelve miles.

The other route leaves Keswick on the B5289 going westwards, turning left onto the main A66 for just under half a mile before turning left again into the pretty village of Portinscale. Follow this minor road southwards taking the right fork to Swinside and Stair after a mile or so. Park at the Swinside Inn for a few moments and take in the southerly view of the lovely Vale of Newlands and the fells around it. Drive on down to Stair and follow the road beneath Causey Pike up into the gentle pass below the Derwent Fells to Newlands Hause then dropping down to Buttermere. Turn left into the lakeside road and drive up to the Gatesgarth car park. If you are based at Keswick, whichever route you take to get to Gatesgarth, take the other one back. This very fine circular trip is known as the 'Buttermere Round' and it gave many early tourists to the Lakes their first glimpse of the power and the beauty of the landscape here, and thankfully, nothing has happened to change that.

The Walk

From Gatesgarth walk up the road towards Honister for about 100 yards, turning off at the wide stone path on your right.

Leave this almost immediately to take the grassy slopes off to your left aiming for the clear path up the ridge that is now directly in front of you.

Take the shale path around the white memorial cross, "Erected by the friends of Fanny Mercer accidently killed 1887". If you want you can stop off to examine this simple inscription by taking the short path that leads up to it.

Follow the path around and above the memorial. Rocky and steep the loose shale here can be quite

Fleetwith Pike from near Gatesgarth

treacherous after heavy rain and the substantial erosion that has occurred in some places here suggests careful footwork under any conditions.

Take the steep right hand fork in the path just above the white cross, clambering up to the grassy mound on top of Low Raven Crag. Here you can pause to take in the heather clad slopes of the slightly intimidating Fleetwith Edge with your onward path clearly visible. To the north west, even at this early stage, are some lovely views over Gatesgarth Farm, Buttermere and Crummock Water. Under the right conditions this is a view which no walker/photographer should miss. It is simply one of the finest and most easily attained views in Lakeland, and if this is as far as you want to go on this particular walk you would not regret it.

Continue up the convenient grassy steps to start the ridge climb proper, enjoying the dark crags and screes of Haystacks off on your right and the great glacial scoop of Honister Pass on your left.

Look out for lovely heather here in late summer clinging to the rocky slopes as the grass gives way to the shale path that winds its way over the ridge.

This is a true ridge walk and there are many stopping points where you can enjoy the views on every side. The final lap to the top is steep, quite exposed and exciting, with the silent Gatesgarthdale Beck meandering its way down Honister far below as you hoist yourself over the last few rocks to the summit.

Vale of Newlands with Newlands Church

Here, from the pointed, witches-hat of a cairn, many famous Lakeland peaks can be seen, the Gables and Windy Gap, Kirk Fell, Haystacks, now below you, the dark fortress of Pillar, Robinson, Hindscarth, Dale Head, and the scattered rocks of Grey Knotts rising casually from the Honister quarry.

The summit is grassy with lots of space to explore the pathway along the edge of Honister Crag that eventually drops down past the quarries and spoil heaps to join one of the disused tramway routes down to the cutting shops and public showroom of the Buttermere and Westmorland Green Slate Company.

Bear left out of the quarry onto the road, through the great slate 'gateway' and down into Honister itself, enjoying a leisured, pedestrian-eye view of this magnificent pass back down to Gatesgarth, a round trip of just under four miles.

As you walk down through the pass you might like to contemplate the great towers of rock that rise up on your left, and which only moments ago you were striding across and which Walpole in *Rogue Herries* chooses as the spot for Francis Herries to meet his destiny.

Fleetwith Pike from the track to Haystacks

Dale Head - 2,473 ft (753 metres)

By Bus

Use the No. 79 Keswick to Seatoller service, alighting at Seatoller and taking the 1½ mile walk up to Honister Hause using the tarmac road or the grassy pathways, that nearer the top run alongside it.

By Car

Drive along the B5289 to the car park down behind the Youth Hostel at the top of Honister Pass.

The Walk

Starting opposite the Youth Hostel at Honister Hause this straightforward walk of 1¼ miles ascends just 1,300 ft over fairly gentle terrain to the cairn at the top of Dale Head. The path is easy, following as it does a fence nearly all the way to the top; it is a bit longer than it looks from the bottom,

Honister Crag

and although not the most interesting walk for attendant views, it does provide a clear prospect of Grey Knotts and the quarry workings around Honister Crag.

There is nothing commonplace about the view from the summit however, which offers a magnificent, full-length prospect of the beautiful Vale of Newlands, while below the Dalehead Crags some of the old mine workings that provide this area with so much of its history and fascination can be picked out against the fellside.

The exhilerating ridge walk to the north-west along Hindscarth Edge from the top of Dale Head is well worth-while, taking the path off to the right that goes up to the big northern cairn on the summit of Hindscarth itself. The view from here offers yet another opportunity for photographers to capture a slightly different perspective of the fine panorama over Newlands, the Vale of Keswick, and the ever- present Skiddaw.

I would recommend that you do continue your walk on to Hindscarth, returning by the same route.

This is another example of a high level walk where some exciting viewpoints are reached quite easily and without too much effort.

To some, of course, my extolling of the easy or quick way up is heresy, for them only exhaustion should be rewarded with such fine prospects.

I take a different view, especially when carrying heavy photographic equipment.

Walpole had some of his characters in *Vanessa* moving over Dale Head, Hindscarth and Robinson as if they were pimples on the landscape, the reality is something different, and the distances covered so easily in one or two pages of a novel might take one or two hours in practice.

I suspect that Walpole guessed some of the distances involved in the perambulations of one or two of his Herries characters. Looking up from the valley below and visualising an interesting journey along some attractive ridges was perhaps an understandable piece of author's licence, and suggests that we should not take the detail and timing of all Herries journey's too seriously.

The 'Witches Hat' cairn on the summit of Fleetwith Pike

Robinson and Hindscarth from Fleetwith Pike

Crosthwaite, Keswick and Greta Hall

Crosthwaite Church

In the year A.D.553 Saint Kentigern, (or Saint Mungo as he was known in Scotland), the patron saint of Glasgow, is said to have planted his cross at a spot about one mile north-west from Keswick. Thus Crosthwaite, 'the clearing of the cross' became the site of the first Christian church in the district, and, strangely enough, although well out of the town centre today, it served as the ancient parish church for Keswick, drawing its congregation from the town itself, and from the farthest limits of the surrounding valleys.

The long distances travelled by some of the worshippers every Sunday probably encouraged them to take some foodstuffs and other surplus items with them to Great Crosthwaite, in the hope of selling or exchanging them. So successful was this mixture of the spiritual and the secular that in the late 13th century a thriving and illegal Sunday market had developed around the church. By 1306 the people of Cockermouth found this success a little too hard to live with, and petitioned parliament on the grounds that the illegal market at Great Crosthwaite was injurious to their own

market trading. They were successful, and the spontaneous market around the church was soon suppressed. Something of a pyrrhic victory this for the people of Cockermouth as the most likely beneficiary of their legal costs would be the thirty year old market at Keswick, which from this date onwards grew from strength to strength.

It does not take a great leap of the imagination to picture the throngs of early fourteenth century illegal marketeers, relieved of their spiritual obligations, chattering and haggling away in the lea of the church, a pragmatic blending of life and litany, commerce and communion.

The Victorians desired something a little more formal in the way of spiritual ambiance, none more so than Robert Southey who was a regular worshipper here after he moved to Greta Hall. He is buried in the churchyard together with many members of his household. A white marble monument showing the poet asleep stands inside the church, complete with a rather long-winded epitaph composed by Wordsworth, who changed the last two lines after they had been carved; a

77

close inspection reveals the amendment.

Canon Rawnsley, vicar of Crosthwaite for 34 years, a founding father of the National Trust in 1895, and a tireless worker in the early days of Lakeland conservation, is also buried here.

The present church is the fourth to have stood on this site, and with Skiddaw almost growing out of its churchyard it must be one of the most beautiful and interesting religious sites in the Lake District.

Walpole knew Crosthwaite and its church well. Here he sited 'Westaways' the fictional home of Pomfret Herries the well-to-do brother of the 'Rogue', a fine house with formal gardens and orange trees reaching down to the shallows and rushes on the northern shores of Derwentwater.

Walpole teases us on the supposed location of this fine family residence; he gives his readers just enough information to stimulate their curiosity, without their ever being able to completely satisfy it.

In *Rogue Herries* young David takes in the view from the windows of the house:

Southeys' Grave

"He was indeed enchanted with the softness and beauty of everything. Beyond the wide window he could see the trim hedges, the paved path, the fountain with a strange stone bird, long-necked and violent-beaked, rising out of it, and beyond the fountain the line of trees guarding the waters of the lake."

Walpole uses Westaways as an important symbol of the developing affluence and power of one branch of the Herries family during the first two novels, *Rogue Herries* and *Judith Paris*, utterly different from the simple gardens and dairies of the Herries at Fell House in Uldale. The tension that develops from these different life styles tumbles over into the third novel *The Fortress*, where the two branches of the family become hopelessly divided and locked into feud. In *The Fortress* Walpole re-caps on the origins of the house, how old Pomfret Herries sought to go one better than his neighbours and employed the aged architect John Westaway to build him something distinctive that would bring credit to the Herries name:

"It was situated between Crosthwaite church and the town of Keswick. At that time the gardens ran down to the fringe of the lake. The virtues of the house were its beautiful tiles of rosy red, the delicate wrought-iron work across its front, the sash windows at that time a great rarity - the pillared hall, and especially the saloon, whose decorations were designed and executed by John Westaway himself. The subject of the design was Paris awarding the apple, and the three goddesses were painted with extreme vigour."

Standing on the north shore of Derwentwater, near the modern camping site, we can imagine, as Walpole did, this fine house standing somewhere between us and Crosthwaite Church, its sash windows catching the last rays of the sun as it dropped behind the craggy contours of Borrowdale.

In *The Fortress* a brief note, almost an aside, tells us that Westaways was pulled down in the autumn of 1836, ostensibly to make room for some alms houses. A similar fate befalls the fictional Fell

Keswick and Skiddaw from Castle Head

House at Uldale, which also disappears in *Vanessa* as a result of a devastating fire.

Perhaps this is Walpole's way of telling us not to look too deeply for signs of the Herries.

He imagined some of their houses, and, in his imagination, he pulled them down again. They never existed, they were never meant to be traced, a sort of public secret, to keep us guessing.

Not so with Keswick, lying between two lakes, Bassenthwaite to the north and Derwentwater to the south, 'Kesewic', (the old name literally meant 'a cheese dairy') sits in an open valley on the River Greta amid some of the most breathtaking scenery in Cumbria. The town developed slowly and only began to expand towards the end of the thirteenth century when Thomas de Dertwentwater successfully petitioned Edward I in 1276 to grant a charter allowing a Saturday market in the town.

There is still a thriving market held every Saturday in Keswick that certainly does not look over seven hundred years old, and where it is still possible to pick-up early editions of Walpole's Herries books for a few pounds.

It was in the mid-sixteenth century, however, that things really began to happen in the town. In 1561 Queen Elizabeth I made an agreement with one Daniel Hechstetter setting up the 'Company of Mines Royal', which, with the aid of skilled German miners imported from the Bavarian Tyrol, was to seek out ores of gold, silver, copper and mercury in the Keswick district, the Virgin Queen taking ten per cent of everything discovered.

It is perhaps fitting that Keswick, bounded on all sides by such a powerful landscape should owe its modern existence to what could be drawn and dragged from the very rock and crags around it.

The Germans mined mainly at Newlands. Not the most welcome of immigrants in this fiercely

79

insular country, they lived for a time detached from the local population, on Derwent Island on Derwentwater.

Love and courtship, of course, are generally no respectors of linguistic and national barriers, and bridges of friendship were soon built across the prejudice and suspicion. Considerable intermarriage brought a new vocabulary to the parish registers. Indeed the records of Crosthwaite Church suggests international harmony on a grand scale recording no fewer than 176 children by German fathers between 1565 and 1584. Perhaps the Germans passed on some of their mining skills to other members of the community. They certainly shared their prosperity with the tradespeople of Keswick, and after the mindless destruction of the smelting equipment at Brigham by Cromwellian soldiers in 1648, (almost a hundred years after the mining had begun), the town's fortunes fell into decline.

The famous Borrowdale graphite mines above Seathwaite gave the town a new lease of industry towards the end of the eighteenth century with the manufacture of pencils. The pencil factories were set by the fast flowing River Greta, from which they gained their power. The old mine workings continued until the late 1860s, and the pencil factories themselves until the 1930s when a modern pencil factory was built, and fine Rexel pencils are still made in the town today, without a trace of the local material which started the whole business off.

Keswick is, in many ways, the dramatic nexus of all four 'Herries' novels. Here many of the meetings, fairs, and feasting in which all the Herries clan took such delight were set, and the town is a vital staging post for both their business and their pleasure.

Francis Herries' elder brother, Pomfret, lived here, at Westaways, not far from the lake near Crosthwaite Church; the meadows nearby provided the setting for the lively 'Chinese Fair' where *Rogue Herries* sold his troublesome mistress Alice Press to a Mr. Rosen:

"The fair was on the farther side of Keswick, on the broad meadows that ran to the lake's edge, not far from Pomfret's grand house, and it pleased Francis to think how greatly Pomfret must dislike to have all this rapscallion world at his very door."

It was to her uncle Pomfret's house in keswick that Mary Herries went to live when she could no longer tolerate the rough and ready life of the house in Borrowdale, eventually marrying Pomfret's sickly son Raisley Herries and moving to London. Little wonder she hastened away; in *Rogue Herries* Walpole paints a less than romantic picture of the eighteenth century town:

"Keswick at this time was a town of one fair street and a huddle of filthy hovels. In the minor streets and 'closes' the cottages, little houses and pigsties were thronged very largely with a foreign and wandering population — riff-raff of every sort who came to steal plumbago from the mines or were wandering their way northward, off the main route; these houses were crowded with foul middens and encroached on by large open cesspools, pigsties and cow-sheds. The refuse stagnated and stained the air and tainted the soil. Here were women of ill fame, hucksters, thieves, many Jews who paid high prices for the stolen lead. At once on entering the town you were in another world from the honest and independent country statesmen and yeoman of the valleys — these statesmen who for centuries had lived on their own land, their own masters, and owed no man anything".

Nowadays the modern visitor is not looking to fill up his car with stolen graphite, and the ladies at the Tourist Information Centre in the old Moot Hall rarely get enquiries about the 'foul middens', or the 'women of ill-fame'. Today's concerns are 'the weather on the fells', ' the times of the motor launch service on the lake', and avoiding a parking ticket in the town centre.

The forty odd years since Walpole's death have seen a dramatic increase in seasonal visitors to the town, now one of the most popular tourist centres in the Lake District. Walpole's eighteenth century vision is difficult to sustain among so many bright hats and anoraks, but it is still quite

A launch on Derwentwater

small, still intimately linked with the lake at its side, and still another world away from the valleys and fells around it.

Keswick has never attracted attention on the scale of Grasmere for its literary associations, but Greta Hall in Keswick, the home of Samuel Taylor Coleridge for nearly four years, and of Robert Southey for forty years, was as much a centre of the 'Lake Poets' menage as Dove Cottage or Rydal Mount.

Coleridge was the first to live here, bringing his wife and son Hartley to Greta Hall in 1800. He had already written 'The Ancient Mariner' (blamed by Wordsworth for the poor sales of the first edition of 'The Lyrical Ballads' in 1778, because no-one seemed to understand it), 'Kubla Khan', 'Frost at Midnight' and almost all his other great poems. He shared the house, or rather the two houses beneath one roof, with his landlord, a Mr Jackson, and his four years here were not particularly

happy ones for Coleridge.

While here he wrote 'Ode to Dejection', probably his last poem of any importance, which signalled his deep sadness at the fruitless search for solace among abstruse metaphysical research.

His rheumatism and pains in the head became worse and more frequent while he was here, and his habit of using laudanum (a compound of opium), to relieve the pain became fixed while he was at Greta Hall. He always protested that the habit was solely due to his need to overcome physical pain and not 'any craving after pleasurable sensations', and he became very bitter and miserable as he contemplated his growing addiction to the drug. In April 1804 he sailed for Malta and 'an even and dry climate' in a bid to halt the decline in his health and to lift his spirits. His wife and children were left at Greta

Hall under the protection of the easily burdened Southey.

Southey's wife was sister to Sarah Coleridge and in 1803 the Southey family moved into Greta Hall, taking occupancy of the other 'house within the house'. Coleridge had for all intents and purposes abandoned his family in 1804, (although he did leave his wife the revenue from an annuity that was his sole source of regular income), and Southey courageously took on their care and maintenance; "to think how many mouths I must feed out of one inkstand". Despite these burdens Greta Hall was to prove a congenial setting for Southey's multifarious writings. he was a prolific contributor to the Quarterly Review, he published a classic 'History of Brazil' as part of an uncompleted history of Portugal (the Brazilian goverment financed the restoration of his grave at Crosthwaite Church in 1961), he also completed a 'Life of Nelson' and much epic poetry on ancient and exotic mythologies. He often wrote for his children penning an oft quoted 'fun' poem on the Lodore Falls, and creating 'Who has been eating my porridge?' as the author of the Three Bears. In 1813 on Sir Walter Scott's generously passing it over, Southey was made Poet Laureate. He accepted it on condition that he might be excused the drudgery of composing birthday odes.

Walpole enjoyed setting Herries characters alongside real historical personalities, particulary literary ones. In *Rogue Herries* the 'Rogue' himself has a private audience with Bonny Prince Charlie in Carlisle in 1745; and in the same novel Deborah Sunwood, after moving to Cockermouth, becomes a friend of the Wordsworths.

In *Judith Paris* Judith meets Sir Walter Scott in Paris, and after moving back to Uldale in 1809 she goes to tea with Mrs Southey at Greta Hall, listening to some gossip on the way:

> "They say that Mr Coleridge dislikes his wife extremely and will never again return to Keswick. He goes often, I believe, to visit Mr Wordsworth at Grasmere".

At Greta Hall she is given a tour around the house:

> "Much good furniture, Mr Southey's writing

table piled with books and papers, a screen, a desk. The room was decorated in quiet dignified tones, the curtains of French grey merino, the furniture covered with some buff colour. A noble room, the room of a poet, lit now with the summer sun, and all the summer sounds mingling beyond the open window."

Southey lived at Greta Hall until his death in 1843; he would no doubt be gratified that today it serves as part of Keswick School, where learning and literature still play an important part in the life of the house.

How to get there

Maps

Outdoor Leisure Map O.S. 1:25,000 N.W. sheet and O.S. 1:50,000 (pink covers) sheet 90 Penrith and Keswick and sheet 89 West Cumbria.

By Bus

There are many bus services that include Keswick on their routes e.g. to and from Penrith, Workington, Cockermouth, Carlisle and Ambleside.

By car

Keswick is easily reached by car on the A66 from Workington, Cockermouth or Penrith, and at the northern end of the A591 from Windermere via Ambleside and Grasmere.

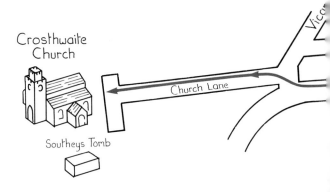

The Walk

Keswick and Crosthwaite starting from the Fitz Park Museum, Keswick.

This simple walk, taking in the museum, St John's Church, the Moot Hall, Greta Hall and Crosthwaite Church is just the formalisation of many different ways to explore Keswick and its environs. Its only claim is that it includes some of the features associated with Walpole or his novels, that have been mentioned in this book.

Start by a visit to the Fitz Park Museum, Station Road, Keswick, situated on the edge of the Fitz Park itself and on the northern side of the River Greta. This is part of the Fitz Park Trust founded in 1882 to furnish both a recreation ground and a museum of curiosities for the good folk of Keswick. It is full of interesting bits and pieces including the Richardson family's musical stones collected from Skiddaw during the first half of the nineteenth century, and a painting of the vilely used Beauty of Buttermere. Here also, under covers, are Walpole's original manuscripts of each of the Herries novels, and a note-book in which he jotted down chapter headings, historical events,

character outlines, notes on plot development etc. All of these, beautifully bound in leather by Walpole, and donated to the museum by his brother Robin, are available for inspection on application to Mr Norman Gandy, the Curator of the museum since 1968.

The museum also houses a major collection of manuscripts and letters associated with Robert Southey, including material from Wordsworth and Ruskin, again most of this stored away for safe keeping and can be examined on request to the curator.

Leave the Fitz Park Museum crossing over the river into Station Street and towards the centre of town. Turn right into St John Street and follow this past the old school buildings to St John's Church which is reached by a small alleyway just off on your right. Built of sandstone in 1838 by a Leeds industrialist, this is the church that Walpole used regularly later on in his life and where he asked to be buried. His grave is marked by a celtic cross on the western side of the church just above the wall that separates the top and the bottom parts of the graveyard. Standing by the grave you can take in

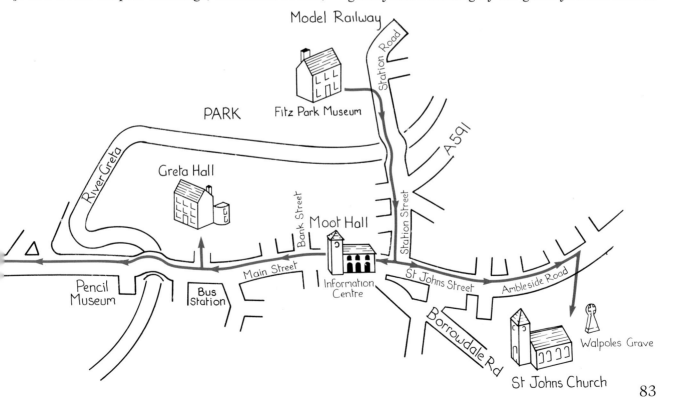

83

some pleasant views of Cat Bells and Causey Pike much as Walpole himself did when he planned his last resting place.

From here re-trace your steps down St John Street to the Moot Hall. Completely re-built in 1813 when the old market square court house was pulled down, it is said that stones taken from the ruined manor of the Radcliffe family on Lord's Island were used in the new construction, which is now Keswick's most famous landmark. Today it houses the Tourist Information Office.

From the Moot Hall make your way down Main Street to Keswick School which can be seen off on your right as you leave the main shopping area. At the top of the school's tarmac drive stands Greta Hall, built by a prosperous carrier who sought to retire with his books, it was first the home of Coleridge and then Southey. Looking at the two plaques near the main door that record their times here, it is not difficult to imagine the two households, two sisters, two poets, hordes of children and piles of books all packed into this pleasant three-storied house on its grassy knoll, full of chatter, learning, and some darkness before Coleridge left for Malta towards the end of 1803.

Now part of the school its interior can only be viewed on request, this and a walk around its exterior is probably best left to the quiet of the school holidays. Leaving Greta Hall, turn right out of the school drive and follow Main Street westwards over the bridge into High Hill, past the Pencil Museum on your left and out of the town eventually bearing right into Church Lane which leads up to Crosthwaite Church.

The present church dates from 1523, although the roof and seating date from the extensive restoration carried out under the direction of Sir Giles Gilbert Scott in 1844. Robert Southey's grave is well signposted and can be found on the north-west side of the tower, a simple, plain, table-top tomb set among some of the finest scenery in England.

Before returning to Keswick, enjoy a stroll with your camera in the churchyard or in the fields around the church to take in the splendour of Skiddaw from this particular vantage point.

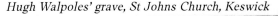

Hugh Walpoles' grave, St Johns Church, Keswick

Greta Hall, Keswick the home of Coleridge and Southey

Derwentwater and Cat Bells

Derwentwater and Watendlath

Derwentwater

Looking south from the north shore of Derwentwater towards the jaws of Borrowdale on a misty day, or across the lake towards Cat Bells in fading light on a summer's evening, no-one can be surprised at Hugh Walpole's choosing this lake as the epicentre for his great Cumbrian saga.

From his library and writing room at Brackenburn on its south west corner he was witness to all its moods; the ceaseless change of colour, the tumbling cloud formations throwing great jigsaw puzzles of dark over the lake and the fells around it, the storms, the unpredictable mists, and the immaculate reflections on those rare and wonderful days when the lake is a mirror to everything around it.

The waters that feed the lake also come down from some of the most romantic sources in the northern fells; Sty Head, Langstrath, the high becks that run off Glaramara and Honister, all touched by Walpole in his stories and all merging together in Borrowdale to become the River Derwent. The rain that falls on the Watendlath fells also finds its way to Derwentwater, flowing by way of the Watendlath tarn, and then over the falls at Lodore.

Derwentwater has so many features, striking scenery, classic viewpoints, bays and landing stages, woods and islands, that it is almost invidious to pick out 'bits' without mentioning them all. One of my own favourite spots is the view from the Portinscale-Grange road on the western shore, looking down on Brandelhow Bay and the boat-houses there, and across the lake to Castlerigg Fell. The colours here in the autumn are stunning, and the woodland footpath below here is well worth exploring.

Brandelhow Park nearby was the first piece of land in the Lake District to be bought by the National Trust. That was in 1902; the Trust now own almost 6,000 acres here and in Borrowdale including most of the western shore, all of the islands and the rocky headland of Friars Cragg on the eastern shore. This latter viewpoint is probably the most famous in lakeland, and justly so. It prompted John Ruskin (first Slade Professor of Art at Oxford), who later had a house near Coniston Water, to write:

> "The first thing I remember as an event in life being taken by my nurse to the brow of Friars Crag on Derwentwater; the intense joy, mingled with awe that I had in looking through the mossy roots, over the crag, into the dark lake".

For the Herries clan the lake and its environs generally symbolised relaxation and pleasure, as on the occasion of the famous summer fair of 1827 in *The Fortress*:

> "Mrs Bonadventure, attended by husband and friends, was soon seated like a queen on the commanding perch of Friars Crag... Very soon the borders of the lake were thronged with figures, and the water whispered with the soft splash of oars. Across the meadows and the trees suddenly broke out the bells from Crosthwaite, and

Evening light on Derwentwater behind Friars' Crag

from the landing-stage the blast of the Town Band. A gun was fired on the Island; the Fete was begun.

In *Judith Paris* at a firework display on Derwentwater arranged by the eccentric Joseph Pocklington, (a real character who built a range of odd buildings during the 1770s on Derwent Isle, including a church, a fort, a battery and a mock 'Druid's Circle'), the twelve year old Judith is beguiled by Georges Paris during a secret sortie on the lake:

> "Fires were burning now on Vicars Island, the set pieces of the fireworks. A trellis-work of flame ran like live things from tree to tree. All the lake near the island glowed, but in the

Keswick landing stages, Derwentwater

distance it was very dark, with a smokey sheen on it, the first fore-shadowing of the moon".

Rowing boats can still be hired from near the Keswick landing stages, and for the less energetic the scheduled 'Keswick Launch' motor boat service does a round trip of all the pick-up points on the shore, but 'fireworks' would probably require a prior arrangement.

Watendlath

There can hardly be a hamlet and a tarn in the Lake District that is visited more, or photographed more than Watendlath. A must for every calendar, (Watendlath is magical in the snow), the tiny cluster of cottages by the small tarn cradled between Thirlmere and Borrowdale provides one of the supreme visual experiences of the northern lakes.

Linked to Derwentwater by the Watendlath Beck which drops nearly 600 feet before it joins the lake, Watendlath is connected to Borrowdale by the narrow road which joins the main valley at Ashness Gate, near Barrow Bay on the eastern shore of Derwentwater. Cars can be taken up this road but the walk up through the Ashness Woods provides the mildly energetic with a succession of wonderful viewpoints, particularly from the packhorse bridge at Ashness and from the steep cliffs of Surprise View.

The more adventurous can explore the crags that leave the woods and descend steeply down the valley. The rocky paths that lead up through these from the Lodore Falls provide a slightly more challenging route to the hamlet for those who prefer to feel that they are really climbing.

Yet another approach is the path up from the Hazel Bank Hotel, (the site of 'Rogue Herries' house), at Rosthwaite. Visitors can park their cars in the car park at Rosthwaite, walk across the bridge and turn left just before the hotel. This path over the shoulder of Brund Fell, although quite steep at first, is well marked and the mile-long journey is quite manageable for walkers of all ages. The views back towards the western and southern walls of Borrowdale are quite breathtaking, and, once over the fell and descending directly down to Watendlath, the whitewashed cottages clustered around the reed-strewn corner of the tarn form an unforgettable memory of this idyllic spot.

Walpole was smitten by the beauty of this place, and here he made a home for his most famous heroine, Judith Paris. In the novel of the same name she comes to live here for a time with her smuggler husband, Georges Paris; she loved it and became part of it. Later on, although longing to return here and live in seclusion, she is prevented by the intensity of the family feuds which surround the Herries at Uldale and High Ireby.

The hidden valley gave Georges Paris the secrecy and isolation that he needed to cloak his nefarious

Watendlath covered with snow

Watendlath

dealings out of Whitehaven:

> "Watendlath was an exceedingly remote little valley lying among the higher fells above Borrowdale. It could indeed be scarcely named a valley; rather it was a narrow-strip of meadow and stream lying between the wooded hills, Armboth on the Grasmere side and King's How and Brund Fell on the other."

I have mentioned the dispute that Walpole attempted to settle in 1937 over the exact location of Judith Paris' house. The house is where Georges is eventually killed by being thrown from a stairway, and where Judith spends so many carefree and also desperately unhappy times. Walpole's declaration in 1937 that no one house was chosen is clearly contradicted today, and proves a continuing testament to the tenacity of Walpole's association between character and place in the Herries stories.

We can see why. As a relative prepares to ride down off the fells to visit Judith, Walpole's description is both credible and persuasive:

> "Soon looking down, he saw the odd dumpy shape of John Green House, Judith's home. A queer little place indeed, crouched into the soil as though it feared a blow, its narrow

windows peering blindly on to Armboth Fell that here was split to allow a beck to tumble down the hollow . . . "

The house was L-shaped with a double porch:

"From the 'hallan' or passage there were three doors, one that led into the 'down house' now used for farm purposes, baking brewings and the rest, the second that led to the garden and the third to the 'house-place', or 'house', a beautiful room with lovely views, surrendered now entirely to Judith".

Indifferent to its authenticity, details such as this attracted, (and still does attract), pilgrims in search of a red haired girl who loved and lost here, and for some physical confirmation of her unconquerable spirit.

The National Trust now own Watendlath, retaining it more or less as when Dorothy and William Wordsworth walked by it one hot day in August 1800, "Wattenlath a heavenly scene" Dorothy's journal, and as Hugh Walpole found it one hundred and twenty nine years later. The Wordsworths passed by, to immortalise other Lakeland features in verse, Walpole stopped to give a generation a compelling glimpse of the great beauty of this hanging valley in the fells above Borrowdale.

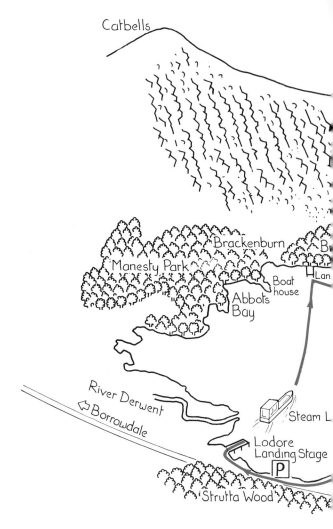

How to get there

Maps

Outdoor Leisure Map O.S. 1:25,000 N.W. sheet, and O.S. 1:50,000 (pink covers) sheet 90 Penrith and Keswick and sheet 89 West Cumbria.

By Bus

There are many bus services that include Keswick on their routes e.g. to and from Penrith, Workington, Cockermouth, Carlisle and Ambleside. The many walks around Derwentwater are just a short step from the bus station in Titheburn street.

By Car

Keswick and Derwentwater are easily reached by car on the A66 from Workington, Cockermouth, or Penrith, and at the northern end of the A591 from Windermere via Ambleside and Grasmere. The B5289 Buttermere, Honister, Borrowdale road to Keswick is a particularly enjoyable way to skirt the eastern shore of the lake, taking advantage of the car parks at the lakeside itself and in the woods near the roadside. There are a number of car parks dotted around Keswick but the most convenient for a walk around Derwentwater is the car park on the Lake road just a short distance from the Keswick landing stages.

The Walks

I have already mentioned the various routes to Watendlath, and the interesting lakeside path that follows the western edge of Derwentwater from Brandelhow Bay to Hawes End at the northern

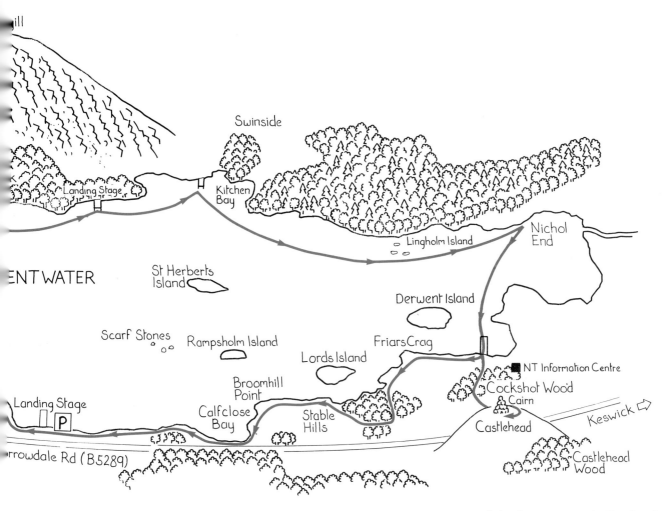

Map labels (reading across the illustration):

Gill

Landing Stage

Swinside

Kitchen Bay

Lingholm Island

Nichol End

ENTWATER

St Herberts Island

Derwent Island

Scarf Stones

Rampsholm Island

FriarsCrag

Lords Island

NT Information Centre

Broomhill Point

Cockshot Wood

Cairn

Landing Stage

P

Calfclose Bay

Stable Hills

Keswick →

Castlehead

rrowdale Rd (B5289)

Castlehead Wood

end of Cat Bells. There are many other walks around Derwentwater, and a close study of the map will no doubt suggest a number of possibilities that you can explore.

1. Around Derwentwater

This easy walk follows the eastern edge of the lake, beginning at the Keswick landing stages and then following the shore path to Friar's Crag. This viewpoint is justifiably famous. Named after the Lindisfarne pilgrims who once embarked here for St Herbert's Island to receive a blessing from the solitary missionary who made his home there, the view across and down the lake must have moved them as it moves us today, a powerful combination of rock and water, light and shadow, mist and woodland, truly one of the finest spots in England.

Take the lakeside path from Friar's Crag above Strahdshag Bay, skirting Ings wood as you move away from the lake and into the wood itself, a straightforward woodland path on to the wooden gate Near Stable Hills. Pass through this and up and over the grassy sward following the small wooden footpath signs down to the lake shore.

Follow the grassy path along the shore to the small tree-covered point at Broomhill (not named on the map) but aptly covered by broom plants on its lakeside slopes. Enjoy the fine views from here — there is a seat — down the lake to the Jaws of Borrowdale and across to Cat Bells and Maiden Moor.

The Watendlath Tarn

The nearest island is Rampsholme, where charcoal-fuelled furnaces once smelted the iron ore torn from the local mines, and which now provides a roost for a number of Cormorants who can sometimes be seen dipping and diving off Broomhill and the Scarth Stones just to the south of the island.

As you follow the path around Calfclose bay, another gentle cove much favoured by visitors to Derwentwater, you can get a clear impression of the size and shape of Walla Crag and its rocky neighbour Falcon Crag rising directly in front of you above the Borrowdale road. Follow the path through the trees, whose roots have been exposed by the constant lapping of the lake waters, eventually climbing up above the lakeside on a path that gets narrower, among roots and rocks, and which is badly eroded in some places. The path follows the line of the Borrowdale road eventually dropping down to the attractive Ashness Gate landing stage. From here continue around the shore to the gate leading into the meadow at the southern tip of Barrow Bay, walk across this and then make your way up to continue your walk on the road itself. After a few yards of road-walking you can turn into an attractive lakeside car park, for a picnic, a rest, or just to feed the ducks; a bit crowded in high summer but almost deserted in autumn and winter time.

From here a brisk walk along the road, or preferably, on the lovely woodland pathway through Strutta and Low Crag woods on the opposite side of the road, brings you to the gate

Derwentwater from Brandelhow

Cutting through the smooth surface of the lake

that leads down to the Lodore landing stage, right next to the heavily silted-up entrance of the River Derwent into the Lake.

There are seven landing stages served by the Keswick-on-Derwentwater Launch Company, from British Summer Time in March until the first Sunday in November. They call at all the stages *on request* (so look conspicuous) sailing both clockwise and anti-clockwise around the lake from Keswick. Timing your arrival at any one of the landing stages is simply a question of obtaining a copy of the current timetable. If you can wait for a clockwise running ferry at the Lodore landing stage it will most probably call at all four of the stages on the western side of the lake before bringing you back to Keswick, a pleasant way to end your walk-cruise around Derwentwater.

2. Castle Head

If the day is fine, and if you have the time after your circuit of Derwentwater, you might explore the short walk beginning at the stone steps just past the National Trust Information Centre.

Climb these and take the path straight ahead through Cockshot wood, bearing right towards the fence and then taking the left fork where the path divides.

Follow this path down out of the wood to the straight narrow track that runs across a field between wire fences.

At the end of this path take the concrete steps up to the small stone wall alongside the B5289 Keswick to Borrowdale road. Cross over here, carefully as it can be very busy in summer, and climb up through the very narrow steps in the stone wall directly opposite, through the wooden swing gate and up the dirt path into Castlehead wood. Walking up the slope among the trees, make your way to the simple wooden bench with three M's cut into the side of it, bearing right up to the clearly marked pathway to the rocky sides of the summit. A variety of 'scrambles' give access to the top where two seats await you, and a fixed stone cairn with a steel plate giving the direction of significant features will also be found.

The views from here are something of a surprise given that it only takes fifteen minutes to get here from the side of the lake and that you are at a height of only 444ft (162 metres).

Many thousands of years ago this little tower of dolerite pushed itself up through a weak point in the soft slate of the valley floor to provide a natural platform for today's walker and photographer. Offering a magnificent view of all the main fells around Derwentwater and Borrowdale this easily achieved 'grandstand' should not be missed.

Derwentwater from Castle Head

Skiddaw from Surprise View

Skiddaw, Skiddaw House and the Castlerigg Stone Circle

At 3054 feet Skiddaw is the fourth highest peak in England, just 152 feet less than Scafell Pike. Its benign slopes dominate Keswick, indeed, they seem to rise from the very streets of the town. For geologists it epitomises the laying down, in a long lost shallow sea, of the ancient Skiddaw Slates, the soft and geologically very old mud-rocks whose smoothly rounded shoulders cover much of the northern fells.

As well as being one of the oldest, Skiddaw is one of the most well-known and most loved peaks in the Lake District. Possibly more interesting to look at than to climb, it does offer a magnificent view across Derwentwater from just below its summit.

The prospect of Skiddaw from near Ashness Bridge must be one of the best remembered views in England, anyone with a camera has to be out of film to resist it.

At Brackenburn, Walpole could watch the changing moods and colours of Skiddaw from his study window, and it becomes a constantly recurring reference point in all the Herries novels.

It is never far from life in Borrowdale, Uldale or Keswick, a silent witness to all Herries doings; to their movements back and forth around the lake to their fortunes, good and bad, to their councils, wise and wasteful. Skiddaw stands perhaps as a symbol of a similar continuity, its colours and hues always changing, yet its ancient rocks fixed and immutable, just as the more ambitious Herries wish their family to be.

Walpole was very sensitive to the effects of the changing light on the fells, and Skiddaw's great bulk reflects many variations, as on the way to a ball at Keswick in *Rogue Herries*,

> "As they rode through Portinscale village over the stream by old Crosthwaite Church into Keswick (the shadow of Skiddaw, russet and silver-grey, sprawling above them), he fell into thought".

And again in *Rogue Herries* as the backdrop to the great football game on the downs above Fell House in Uldale:

> "... the sloping backside of Skiddaw catches the light; it is as though it rolled its coat off and spread there basking, while the clouds are shadowed across the shining surface".

The photographer needs lots of patience, some luck, and most of all, the tenacity to pursue his goal in all seasons if he is to catch a representative sample of Skiddaw's many 'coats'.

One and a half miles due east of Skiddaw's summit stands the lonely Skiddaw House, 1600 feet above sea level on a rising hill on the gentle slopes at the 'back o' Skidda'; it must surely be one of the most isolated buildings in England.

When Walpole was writing *The Fortress* in 1930 he would have known the solitary shepherd, Pearson Dalton, who amazingly occupied part of this house for 47 years between 1922 and his retirement at 75 years of age in 1969. Spending

Skiddaw House, scene of the infamous murder in 'The Fortress'

his weekdays here, along with his dogs and 1,000 sheep or so, Pearson would have looked out on Great Calva and the barren tracks of Skiddaw Forest that surround it.

To this spot in *The Fortress* Walpole causes Uhland and John Herries to come one damp, misty day in September, 1854, for a desperate four o'clock rendezvous to:-

> "have it out, the two of us, once and for all - alone".

These two, related by blood but divided by the bitter family feud that has haunted them both since childhood, made their separate ways to the deserted house. John Herries rides from Uldale:

> "He was soon lost in the spaces of Skiddaw Forest. There was no forest here; there had never perhaps been trees; the name was used in the old Scottish hunting sense of place for game . . . He knew that under Lonskill was the house, and at the thought that he was now so near to it a shudder that he could not control took him".

Uhland Herries came from The Fortress itself at High Ireby:-

> "Well, he was moving forward, for not far beyond was the rising hill on which the house stood. Behind the house was a wood, and if Wyndham's keeper should be at home

Castlerigg Stone Circle

they could finish this affair among the trees. No-one would see them on such a day".

They face one another in the empty house, Uhland armed with a gun and choking with anger, murders his unarmed uncle and then kills himself; a fictional murder which lives in local memory as notorious as any that might have been committed in real life, and a virile example of Walpole's skill at matching location and event in the Herries stories.

Walpole's manuscript notes on the Herries novels show that he considered setting this murder sequence near Sprinkling Tarn, in emulation of the struggle of an earlier Herries. However, the eerie location and foreboding landscape around Skiddaw House impressed Walpole so much that its future as the scene of a memorable family murder and suicide was assured.

Before Walpole embarked on his family saga, most readers were familiar with the Lake District through the somewhat idyllic word pictures of the Lake poets, particularly in the writings of William Wordsworth, Samuel Taylor Coleridge and Robert Southey. Although celebrating the natural beauty of the landscape, Walpole is less reverential and more earthy in his approach; the green hills can also be bleak and bare, the placid lakes turbulent and the pastoral calm ripped open by dark clouds and swirling mists. Elements of all these can be encountered on the walk to Skiddaw House.

About a mile to the east of Keswick, on a high and lonely site, lies the Castlerigg Stone Circle. Dragged up here by men around 1500 B.C., these thirty-eight perpendicular stones thrusting out from the ground below Skiddaw and the great mass of Blencathra, and above the gentle Valley of St John's in the Vale, testify to early man's settlement and industry in the Keswick area.

These bronze age men left us no signposts or explanations to tell us why they put these stones there. Perhaps they serve many purposes, religious, legal, political, commercial; all of them social, bringing people together on this spot, surrounded by fells and small settlements, in close communion with the land they sought to master.

During the first two weeks of October 1769 the poet Thomas Gray visited the Lake District and started off the modern tourist industry with his 'Journal in the Lakes'. Ostensibly kept for the benefit of his sick friend Dr Warton who couldn't complete the journey, this one piece of publicity conjured up a land of awesome beauty and mystery which the folks down south just couldn't resist. Gray was taken up to the 'Druids circle' by a local guide, (confirmation that 18th century Cumbrians were quick to recognise the value of their assets to the curious), and, as usual, he was careful to note down in his 'Journal' detailed directions on how to find it:

"I saw a Druid circle of large stones, one hundred and eight feet in diameter, the biggest not eight feet high, but most of them still erect; they are fifty in number above the valley of the summits of Catchidecam (called by Camden Casticand) and Helvellyn, said to be as high as Skiddaw, and to arise from a much higher base."

Twelve stones seem to have disappeared since Gray counted them, but perhaps that was just poetic licence. Forty-nine years later another poet, John Keats, spent a few days in Keswick in the June of 1818. He too made his way up to Castlerigg to take in the 'stones'. Perhaps the early summer weather was bad that year as he casts a similar stone circle in 'Hyperion' in 'dull November':

"A dismal cirque of Druid stones upon a forlorn moor, When the chill rain begins at shut of eve In dull November and their chancel vault The heaven itself, is blinded throughout night".

In contrast Walpole chose a fine August day in *The Fortress* for the famous 1827 Summer Fair at Keswick. Twelve young men line up at Crosthwaite Church in order to race through the town to finish at the Castlerigg Stone Circle. The competition was fierce:

"Will Leathwaite made his spurt. He was ahead; Graham caught him. Graham was ahead. Will was level. The Circle, calm, dignified, gazed indifferently out to Helvellyn and Scawfell and the Gavel. Will threw up his head; he seemed to catch all that country into his heart and, fiercely like a swimmer fronting a terrific wave, flung himself across the string, the winner by a head."

Easily reached by a gentle walk up through Keswick, from Threlkeld, or up from St John's in the Vale, it is not necessary to 'run' to Castlerigg to appreciate its setting; however, its mystery and timelessness are truly enjoyed if you can visit the Circle near sunset or sunrise. At such times poetry seems the natural vehicle for expressing the beauty and solitariness of this ancient place. The warm glow on the stones and the long shadows that they throw on the ground are now as they were then and provide a visual link between us and the men who co-operated together to bring them here three and half thousand years ago.

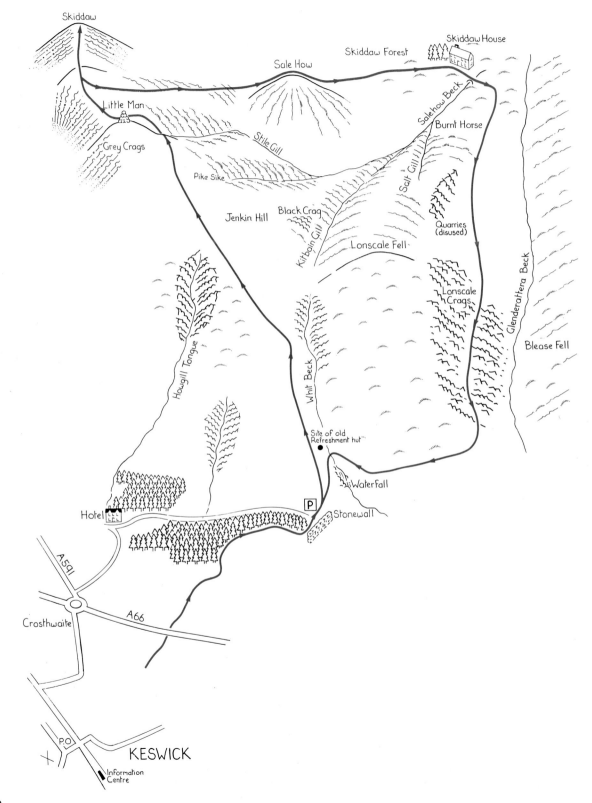

Skiddaw

Sale How

Skiddaw Forest

Skiddaw House

Little Man

Grey Crags

Stile Gill

Salehow Beck

Burnt Horse

Salt Gill

Pike Sike

Jenkin Hill

Black Crag

Lonscale Fell

Quarries
(disused)

Kitbain Gill

Lonscale
Crags

Glenderaterra Beck

Blease Fell

Howgill Tongue

Whit Beck

Site of old
Refreshment hut

Waterfall

Hotel

P

Stonewall

A591

A66

Crosthwaite

P.O

KESWICK

Information
Centre

Great Calva and Skiddaw Forest from Skiddaw House

How to get there

Map

Outdoor Leisure Map O.S. 1:25,000 N.W. sheet Ennerdale and Derwent.

By Bus

Keswick is the best place from which to explore Skiddaw and bus services No. 71 and 35 from Keswick travel along the A591 Carlisle road. Some of the No. 35 services have a scheduled stop at Millbeck Road End from where, by a mixture of road-footpath-road walks, you can reach the Gale Road car park and the beginning of the walk to Skiddaw and Skiddaw House. Alternatively, you can take a bus to Keswick, then make your way up to Briar Rigg and the bridge that crosses the main A66 road into Spooney Green Lane, through Thorny Plats and up along the pleasant walk around Latrigg which eventually comes out at the car park at the end of Gale Road.

By Car

From Keswick town centre make for the large roundabout on the A66 just to the north of Great Crosthwaite. At the roundabout take the A591 Carlisle road, turning off to the right almost at once to follow the minor road up to Ormathwaite and Undersear. At the junction opposite the hotel turn right into the rough road that runs east below Skiddaw's south-eastern slopes, this is Gale Road and it comes to an end at the car park at the back of Latrigg. This car park is just below the 1000ft mark, leaving just over 2000ft to be climbed to Skiddaw, which at 3,053ft is the fourth highest peak in the Lake District.

The path to Skiddaw with the twin peaks of Skiddaw Little and Lesser Man

The Walk

Skiddaw starting from Keswick

From the car park take the obvious path running north-east along the stone wall. Proceed through the gate past the small cross erected in memory of three shepherds, bearing left above Whit Beck, past the site of the old refreshment hut that sustained walkers of a bygone age and on up the popular path to the summit of Skiddaw. This route is quite steep at first but it becomes easier as it crosses over Jenkin Hill, so easy in fact that this becomes a mountain stroll rather than a climb, providing lots of opportunities to photograph the wonderful views south over the Derwent valley which now get better at every step.

Over to the left rise the twin peaks of Skiddaw Little Man and Skiddaw Lesser Man, still a mile away from the main summit, they deserve a visit. The view looking south from the summit of Skiddaw Little Man is breathtaking, a classic Lakeland panorama, taking in Derwentwater and its islands and all the principle Borrowdale fells beyond. It cries out to be photographed. Try using a telephoto lens here and see how some of the detail in this wonderful scene can be taken out and given a new perspective. Before leaving, note the dramatic scree-covered western face of this peak, something of a contrast to the heather and bracken of the route so far.

Walk back down to the main path and begin the gentle slog up to the cairn on the south top, and then on along the stony ridge walk, over another false summit, to the triangulation column at the real summit of Skiddaw. This route up Skiddaw is easy and hospitable to just about everyone who is able to walk, irrespective of age or stamina, however its ease of access sometimes belies the fact that it is a 3,000ft mountain which is bleak and exposed and which can get very, very cold. So, if the temperature is cool down in Keswick, expect it to be bitterly cold on the top of Skiddaw and dress accordingly.

Returning from the summit over south top and down the path to the fence north of Little Man, the possibility of visiting Skiddaw House is an option that might be considered here, depending on the weather and the time of day. If a brisk walk back to Keswick or the Gale Road car park is preferred then that is a simple matter of descending via the broad path used on the way up.

Skiddaw House

From just below south top it is an easy descent down the grassy banks of Skiddaw's eastern slopes to Sale How and then on to the deserted Skiddaw House. Despite the fact that there is no real path, the two miles or so from the fence to the house are easily covered and one is soon in the middle of the wild and desolate space of Skiddaw Forest. The intense quiet, (not many tourists come this way) and haunting beauty of this place are unlike any other experience in the Lakes and we can begin to understand why Walpole set his famous murder and suicide here. There are no trees except for the wind-break plantation to the west of Skiddaw House itself, and the creative photographer will have to juggle with a lot of sky, the imposing pyramid of Great Calva and its patchworks of colour, and the wide open spaces for interesting compositions.

After taking in the atmosphere of this lonely spot a number of options are available to complete your walk. An obvious one is to return to the tourist path on Skiddaw via Sale How and make your way back from there. If, however, you would like to go back by a different route take the path east, down the slopes from Skiddaw House to the wooden bridge over Salehow Beck. Bear right

Castlerigg at sunset

around the slopes of Burnt Horse and along the path south which clings to the sides of Lonscale Fell. Here you are above the Glenderaterra Beck that cuts into the valley between the Skiddaw and Blencathra massifs, and that eventually winds its way into the River Greta. Some parts of the valley below the path are steep and craggy as are parts of Blease Fell opposite which also carries a pathway at about the same height around to the Blencathra Centre and on to Threlkeld.

As you come out on to the southern slopes of Lonscale Fell the views south open up to reveal a magnificent vista of the fells around Derwentwater which, if the light is right, can offer some spectacular photography. Follow the clear path westwards below the fell, crossing the ford by the waterfall, over Whit Beck, and turning south again to walk over the path that you started out on.

Castlerigg Stone Circle

This famous bronze age site is easily reached by a walk up from Nest Brow on the A591 just south east of Keswick. This path runs north almost parallel to Castle Lane and comes out on the western edge of the circle. Alternatively, one can drive east out of Keswick on the A591 through Brigham taking the right fork on to the minor road past High Fieldside to the parking area opposite the gateway to the site.

Uldale

Uldale, Stone Ends, High Ireby, Ireby Old Church, Caldbeck and Hesket Newmarket

The settlements and features of the landscape at the 'back o' Skidda' are probably the least known and least documented parts of the Lake District.

Just within the boundary of the National Park, the workaday villages of Uldale, Ireby, Caldbeck, Hesket Newmarket and Mungrisedale, (Saint Mungo strikes again), often go unnoticed by holiday visitors, and are hardly touched by the crampons of the hard men of the fells who prefer steep slabs to the boggy moorland of Skiddaw Forest or Mungrisedale Common.

In *Rogue Herries* Walpole sets up a rival centre of Herries patriarchy in the tiny village of Uldale, where the Rogue's only son David buys a farm, Fell House, on the hill leading out of the village and leaves the old Herries domain of Borrowdale.

Houses are always important in the Herries novels, Walpole often dwells on the detail of their exterior and interior decoration and furnishing, and the house at Uldale is no exception. Entirely his own creation, half farm, half manor house, with its red brick, dormer windows, trim garden and little orchard it was to become the fulcrum of light and darkness for part of the Herries clan in the next two novels, *Judith Paris* and *The Fortress*:

> "...This was a modern house that had been standing only some ten years or so, charming in spirit and colour, built for comfort rather than display. Above it ran the moor free and unfettered to the skyline, and from that moor you could see behind you the Solway Firth and the Scottish Hills, before you across the valley to Skiddaw, and then, curving to the right, the whole range from Helvellyn through the Pike and the Gavel to Robinson and Grasmoor. Under this glory the house nestled, catching the sun, sheltered from wind and rain."

Here the conservative David Herries would drop like a stone in his garden as his son rejoices in the fall of the Bastille, and from this house in Uldale the young Judith Paris would shin down the water pipe to escape to Stone Ends to join the scandalous Squire Gauntry and his drunken messmates, including the nine year old 'Johnny Peel':

> "Stone Ends, Tom Gauntry's place, was a mile beyond Caldbeck. She made no further encounter. The clock of Caldbeck Church struck seven as she trotted through the deserted little street."

A farm called Stone Ends still stands below Carrock Fell, on the little road off the A66 that leads around the back of Blencathra to Caldbeck and Uldale, its white and green livery quite distinct against the grey rocks rising up to the west of it. I suspect Walpole's version of Stone Ends is very much a mixture of what he found, and what he created:

> "So she arrived at Stone Ends. This was a rough-cast building of no height, with an outside gallery and stair. There were mullioned windows, great trees overhanging the mossy slates and round thick chimneys. There was a garden with a clipped hedge, the fells everywhere beyond, a rough plot of flowers, some outbuildings, a sundial, a little stream."

'Stone Ends'

The present owners owe no blood to the wasteful Gauntry, but the house has been in and out of their family for a generation or so, and, perhaps like the Herries at Uldale, they feel that they too have come home.

Personally, I find that the drive around the back of these northernmost fells, gentle and for the most part undramatic, a pleasant break from the crags and steeps of the south.

Hesket Newmarket, with its old white houses ranged round a slither of village green is a particularly attractive example of one-street calm and serenity. One of the many decayed market centres in the Lake District (nearby Ireby is another), four circular stone pillars of the eighteenth century market cross are all that remain of the trading in sheep and cattle that went on there until the mid-nineteenth century.

Charles Dickens and Wilkie Collins stayed in Hesket Newmarket in 1857, a fine stone dwelling, 'Dicken's House', in the centre of the village is their supposed lodging. They climbed up Carrock Fell and described their excursions in the 'Lazy Tour of Two Idle Apprentices' in Dickens' *Household Words*. Extraordinarily for its size, the village once boasted six inns and a brewery. The latter was operated from the blue and white house which now sports a 'Temperance Hall' sign over

John Peel's grave, Caldbeck

its front door. This strange irony was wrought by a teetotal member of the influential Lawson family who, having enthusiastically emptied his own wine cellars turned on his 'demon' neighbour, and converted it into a 'temple for tea'.

Driven through in seconds, Hesket Newmarket is well worth a few minutes, as is Caldbeck, another pleasant village standing on the northern boundary of the Lake District National Park just twelve miles south of Carlisle. On the map the wide yellow line of the boundary seems to pass over John Peel's grave in Caldbeck churchyard, a graphic irony, as nothing could contain him when he was alive.

Caldbeck is at the centre of John Peel country; he hunted all over these fells, and often celebrated his best days in one of Caldbeck's thirteen inns. The modern huntsman will have to sing 'D'ye Ken John Peel' in the one that now remains or, as the present writer did more than once, enjoy some excellent apple and blackberry pie at the little restaurant almost opposite the church gates.

There are some interesting farm buildings in the village that open straight out onto the main street. There is a clog maker, and the ruins of an early nineteenth century bobbin mill down by the 'Howk', (Cumbrian 'to dig out with a pick or spade') by the River Caldew. A great water wheel turned here where now the river rattles down a small waterfall on its way out of the village only to disappear abruptly somewhere near Parkend, having travelled nearly 14 miles from its source amid the bleak wastes behind Skiddaw near the desolate Skiddaw House.

Uldale itself, (not the prettiest village in the area, and a desolate place to be in the rain), looks at its best from the common just above it. From such a vantage point Walpole, no doubt, painted in his 'Fell House' just below the moors. Attacked by a mob towards the end of *Judith Paris* and burnt to the ground in *Vanessa*, it was the harbour and host to a generation of Herries hopes and aspirations.

Put here by the author's hand, it was eventually crushed by the same pen, as it pencilled in the menace of the dark *Fortress* overlooking it at High Ireby.

Near the end of *Judith Paris*, Judith's nephew and good friend Reuben Sunwood is shot and killed during an attack on Fell House in Uldale by a mob from Cockermouth.

> "Reuben sprang forward, was for a moment illuminated by fire; a shot rang from the road, and he too jumped as though with arms lifted, he would touch the moon, and collapsed on the horse-steps."

The shot was fatal and Reuben was buried five days later in Ireby Churchyard.

Ireby Old Church

At the time Walpole set this incident, (1822), the church serving Ireby would have been this one, some distance away from the village. Indeed, so isolated was it from the easy convenience of the villagers, lying as it does half a mile away up the hill towards Torpenhow, that in 1846 a new parish church was built in the centre of the village. No doubt this increased attendances for worship by making it less hard on the feet.

Walpole would have known of this old church, and it is most certainly where he envisaged Reuben having his last resting place. Bounded entirely by a dry-stone wall and reached only by foot across a field near New Park, this secluded spot fitted in completely with Walpole's picture of Reuben Sunwood, the lonely vagabond preacher, ostracised by his family, distrusted by those whom he harrangued, befriended only by another semi-exiled Herries, Judith Paris.

The twelfth century chancel is all that remains of the old parish church of Ireby. The nave and the north aisle were demolished when the new church was built, and together with the little churchyard, what is left now is maintained by the Redundant Churches Fund.

Not many people trudge across the fields to see it now, those that once did so in earnest have all come and gone. Some of them stayed here under heavy headstones near the fields that they worked, but the marker for Reuben Sunwood is not so easily found.

All authors need a bit of luck as well as talent, and I think it is true to say that Hugh Walpole had a fair share of both. His discovery of The Grange at High Ireby early in 1931, after he had set part of the Herries clan in a farmhouse at Uldale, was the most amazing piece of luck. Here was a stern, Victorian mansion, dark and uninviting, just what he needed to catalyse his ideas and to develop his theme of domination and terror in *The Fortress*. In his manuscript notes for the novel Walpole begins to explore its significance:

> "The Fortress of the title is the Victorian erection of self-confidence, material achievement, courage and strength. By the end of the book it is being assailed on all sides."

At the time Walpole discovered the overgrown gardens and outbuildings of The Grange at High Ireby, it was the real home of James Gurney, who, from his decaying mansion overlooking Uldale, laid claim to most of the farmland around Ireby and Ruthwaite.

The tiny hamlet of Ruthwaite can be seen from the still-remaining walls of The Grange and is noteworthy for a house once said to have been owned by John Peel, and where he is supposed to have died of pneumonia in 1854 at the age of 78.

Gurney died in 1933, the year after *The Fortress* was published, and after his death it seems that The Grange continued to crumble, until in 1956, after some workmen had been burning out dry rot in the roof, a fire began, spread rapidly, and destroyed most of the building. What remained was demolished, the heavy stone carried away, and the Grange was no more.

In the novel, Walter Herries starts the foundations for his grand house in March 1830, but his shadow falls over the family at Uldale before a brick of it was laid, or a stone was cut. Jennifer, alone in her terror is fascinated by the site for the house:

> "So the place was going up, grim and grey and forbidding. its half-grown walls could already be seen from all the country around. . . She was there again, standing on the edge of the rough bare field, her tall black figure framed by the bare hills."

Eventually, the house is completed and the puffed-up Walter insists on a grand ball at which all the 'quality' of the county, and all of the Herries who can stand him, attend.

The drums and violins of the opening ceremonies drift down the valley to Uldale where the distract and bedridden Jennifer is attended by Judith Paris:

> "Judith, her arms about Jennifer, gazed around her desperately for help. But no help could be forthcoming, for with a sigh Jennifer bent her head and falling forward died against Judith's breast."

Walter's powerful gesture of Herries progress and prosperity claims its first victim.

The remains of The Grange at High Ireby, 'The Fortress' in Walpoles' novel of the same name

Caldbeck Church

It is not destined to be a place where much happiness dwells. Walter's only son, the crippled Uhland leaves it to deal a death blow to his uncle and himself at the lonely Skiddaw house, while Walter's beautiful daughter, the serene Elizabeth leaves it for a life of a governess in London, only to return to Cumberland married to her father's arch enemy John Herries of Uldale.

No-one it seems can bear the burden of the house, the price that they have to pay for Walter's pride and the continuance of the Herries feud is too great.

Like the houses in some of Edgar Allen Poe's gothic macabres, the Fortress assimilates the hatred and envy that dwells within it until it becomes a portrait of its owner, twisted and choked, crippled and desolate.

One or two carved fountain heads in the tangled garden, a few stone steps, part of a parapet, and some outbuildings that once housed the laundry are all that remain of the mighty Grange at High Ireby but such is the power of the published word over stone, that even after fifty odd years, *The Fortress* is still read, still lives, is still part of the dark ambition of Walter Herries.

How to Get There

Maps

O.S. 1:50,000 (pink covers) sheet 90 Penrith and Keswick, and the O.S. 1 inch to one mile Tourist Map (illustrated cover).

By Car

Starting from the A66 at Lisco Farm east of Keswick

The only way, other than by an extremely long circular walk to visit the villages and hamlets around the back of Skiddaw is to drive, leaving the car whenever your fancy takes you to explore further. There are no buses serving this area other than the No 71 service which links Keswick with Wigton stopping at Ruthwaite and Ireby.

My approach by car would be from the Penrith side of Keswick, leaving the A66 opposite Lisco farm and driving north along the back road below Souther Fell towards Mungrisdale. Stop here to admire the little church and the small cluster of houses, and possibly the Mill Inn that stand around it.

On to Mosedale taking the turning left below Carrock Fell for a little diversion along a basic road which follows the Caldew and eventually comes to an end near some old mine workings. During the summer this is a holiday place which can be packed with cars bringing bathers to play and relax by the river but in autumn, winter and early spring you are likely to have it to yourself. Parking here provides the opportunity for a number of pleasant walks with a camera, including a track along the Caldew to Skiddaw House and a route to the top of Carrock Fell (2,174 feet) taking care to avoid the holes left over from the disused mine workings.

Back down to the main road press on to Stone Ends, now a lovely farm, directly below the east face of Carrock Fell. Obviously this appealed to Walpole, and the gentle landscape beyond Stone Ends towards Greystoke Forest stands out in strong contrast to the rugged fells above the road.

From here the road crosses some gentle common land to the delightful Hesket Newmarket, certainly worth a walk round, before moving on to Caldbeck and a visit to John Peel's grave in the churchyard there.

From Caldbeck follow the road west out past Parkend, taking the left fork to Uldale where Walpole set so much action in the Herries novels. From here drive north to Ireby, driving through the village and then westwards on the road to Torpenhow calling at the now isolated Ireby Old Church.

From here take the narrow roads south through New Park (peppered with daffodils in the spring) to High Ireby, the site of *The Fortress*. From here note the view across Uldale and imagine the Herries clan feuding over who should dominate this gentle vale.

From here you might also take a walk to the small hamlet of Ruthwaite where John Peel's house stands. From High Ireby take the road south to join the A591 at the Castle Inn. From here there is

Ireby Old Church

Ireby

The Fortress

A591

Castle Inn

Ruthwaite
John Peel's House

Uldale

B5299

Uldale Fells

Skiddaw Forest

Skiddaw

Dodd Wood

Lonscale Fell

Braithwaite

Roundabout

KESWICK

BASSENTHWAITE LAKE

Bowscale Fell

Blencathra

A66

Whelpo
Caldbeck

Caldbeck Church

John Peel's Grave

Hesket Newmarket

Caldbeck Fells

Stone Ends

Carrock Fell

Mine

Raven Crags

Mill Inn

Souther Fell

Church

Mungrisdale

Lisco Farm

an easy drive south again past Bassenthwaite Lake, (the most northern lake in the Lake District and the only one without 'mere' or 'water' in its name), under the west side of Skiddaw and on into Keswick.

This is a drive which, although it skirts the high flanks of Skiddaw and Blencathra, really proclaims the gentler side of the Herries landscape.

It takes in villages which many visitors never see and offers the creative photographer a challenge and a change from the rocky crags of the south.

Photography on the Fells

Serious landscape photography takes time. You will need to leave tracks and pathways in search of better viewpoints, weigh up the light, change films and lenses, choose appropriate filters, explore different compositions, concentrate on focusing and the assessment of depth of field.

None of this can be done in a hurry without making mistakes, losing things or just ending up with mediocre photographs. Obviously there will be times when certain conditions, especially near sunset, cannot wait and you have to point and shoot, adjusting things as quickly as possible; often the result is a fine photograph, but in general the landscape photographer is the slowest thing moving on the fells. Getting good pictures takes care and thought and these are generally not compatible with being the first on top.

Force yourself to stop, resist the temptation to miss or pass over a nice shot just because it means pulling off your rucksack yet again to get the gear out. It will be worth it when you are down at 'home' level again. Good light, a particularly fine profile on the horizon, or the reflections in a lake or tarn, may never be the same again, and if they are, you may not be there to catch them.

I always convince myself that I may never come this way again, and that this is my last chance to get a particular shot; it often works.

Paradoxically, having said that, being prepared to return is probably one of the most important disciplines of the serious landscape photographer.

On poorly lit-days, or if the light is at the wrong angle, make a note of the feature and how it might look at a different time of day or at a different season of the year and make a vow to return.

There are probably more so-called rules for landscape photography than for any other kind. These are really of more use to a landscape painter than a creative photographer, and my advice is to take them with a pinch of salt.

Consider yourself to be on a voyage of exploration and discovery, recognising certain features in certain ways that will perhaps be ignored by another. You will eventually develop a way of seeing things that will be independent of rules and regulations, and that says something about you and the way that you find the world. Do not be afraid to see differently from someone else, it would be a dull world if we all took the same photographs in the same way.

The following sections on equipment and technique are pretty basic and are not meant to be prescriptive. They are intended rather to suggest approaches and options that you can experiment with on the way to developing your own particular style and approach.

Equipment

The most important thing about you and your equipment, is that you 'get on' together, that whatever sort of camera you have, you know its possibilities and its limitations. If you go walking alone as I sometimes do, your camera is a companion that you want to feel comfortable with; that is easy to handle, and that responds quickly after a mad scramble in the rucksack.

I have seen many really good photographs taken with simple, and not so simple, compact cameras, whose owners know them well, and match up their camera settings, film type and lighting conditions to the best possible advantage, usually on clear bright days.

The problem with compact cameras is that they often feature automatic exposure control and generally do not have the scope for the subtle exposure correction that can deal with difficult or non-perfect conditions; and just as important for landscape photography, they may not accept the wide range of filters that can compensate for difficult lighting and help turn a failed or an ordinary picture into something more exciting.

In a word they are generally not versatile enough to turn out consistently good pictures under the wide range of conditions often found in the Lake District.

A more flexible candidate for your rucksack is a reliable 35mm single-lens reflex camera (SLR), capable of accommodating interchangeable lenses, or a 35mm viewfinder camera, some of which will also accept different lenses. Rangefinder cameras enjoy the advantage of being lighter than SLRs and perhaps allowing lower hand-held shutter speeds to be used, as their exposure mechanism causes less internal shake'. Unfortunately, good quality rangefinder cameras are often too expensive for most pockets and the range of interchangeable lenses available is generally not as wide as for a popular make of SLR.

I normally use two 35mm SLR camera bodies, although I do not always carry them both with me on assignments, one standard 50mm lens, a 24mm wide angle lens, a 28mm − 85mm zoom lens and a 70mm − 250mm zoom lens. I find that this selection gives me considerable flexibility with regard to angle of view and image size, and if I am really pushed for space or weight I often manage with just the two zoom lenses.

Obviously the search for low weight combined with versatility and economy will eventually lead you to a personal permutation which you feel happy with.

My equipment is expected to pay for itself many times over, but this does not mean that I can waste cash on a posh camera just to look good; it has to work and it does not have to be too expensive. There are many reliable 35mm cameras available to the serious photographer at very reasonable prices now, and a tremendous range of good quality wide-angle and telephoto lenses from camera makers and independent lens manufacturers. Shop around, look at the advertisements in photographic magazines, particularly the second-hand columns, and never buy a camera without handling it first. Ask how dependent it is on battery power; is it just for the meter or does it power other functions like the shutter? Is the lens fitting a popular one and, if not, what range of lenses are available to fit it? Better to ask the questions in a warm, ground level shop than on some cold mountain top two thousand feet away from the nearest photographic dealer.

Lodore Wood

As well as my 35mm equipment I also use a medium format camera for low-level or easy-access photography. This particular camera provides a negative or transparency size of 6 × 4.5cm on 120 roll film, and this large, rectangular image size, (some 2.7 times greater than that of 35mm) is often preferred by publishers who may want to enlarge the image of a photograph considerably for publication.

If you are considering marketing your landscape photographs in future you might consider purchasing a medium format camera to meet the demands of potential clients; if not then a 35mm outfit is likely to meet all your needs. Indeed, with the advanced fine-grain emulsions now available in 35mm film many publishers are beginning to accept that sharp and well-saturated 35mm colour transparencies can meet all but their most exacting needs.

Films

Because I take photographs for reproduction all my colour work is done using colour slide films which publishers prefer.

I use ordinary Kodachrome 64, and Fujichrome 50/18°, 100/21°, and 400/27°, films for my 35mm work. I do not use Kodachrome 25. Despite its slightly better colour saturation and extra-fine grain, I find it too slow for hand-holding in most conditions on the fells. I think that even the most critical observer would be hard pressed to tell the difference between this film and Kodachrome 64, Fujichrome 50 or even Fujichrome 100 ISO films when enlarged to typical book-page size.

Obviously Fujichrome ISO 400/27°, handy though it is, shows some grain especially when used under cloudy or low-contrast conditions, and it is wise to imagine carefully how this might enhance or harm a scene before loading with this emulsion under such circumstances.

For the large format camera I use Kodak Ektachrome ISO 64/19°, 100/21°, and 400/27°, in 120 (15 frames) and 220 (30 frames) rolls, and Fujichrome ISO 50/18°, 100/21°, and 400/27°, in 120 rolls.

A word here about Professional films eg Ektachrome Professional, Kodachrome Professional etc. These films have been manufactured and 'aged' in a way that will provide the user with optimum results as soon as they leave the factory. Ideally they need to be used and processed as quickly after purchase as possible, and if they are stored they should be kept refrigerated at somewhere between −18°C to −20°C.

Amateur films, on the other hand, have not been 'aged' and the manufacturer's assumption is that these emulsions will reach full maturity while in use, ie. they are likely to be kept in cameras and camera bags longer than their Professional counterparts.

My advice is to go for the amateur colour slide films, as they are cheaper, easier to keep, and the image difference between these and the Professional films is so small that the serious amateur would not really tell the difference.

Getting to know how particular films react and behave under particular conditions is quite important. Obviously it takes time and practice before you can get any real idea of film peculiarities and even when you know there may be nothing much you can really do about them.

Watch out for green casts on Kodachrome 64 when exposed under overcast skies. Ektachrome 64 and 400 tend towards blue under the same conditions and where a lot of sky is included in the

frame; you may get a slight pinkish-magenta tinge with Fujichrome 400 when photographing snow scenes and sunsets. Fujichrome 50, particularly good for brightening up scenes in dull or overcast conditions, can be a bit too much of a good thing under very bright light, and natural greens in particular can seem a bit blatant and unreal.

Because there is little opportunity to compensate for wrong exposure of colour slide films, (the film in the camera is the film you see after processing), its exposure is much more critical than that for colour negative film. To get it right, exposure needs to be correct to within half a stop either way. Most colour slide films can cope with slight, underexposure but show no mercy when overexposed. Fujichrome 100 is unusually tolerant in this respect with overexposure to as much as one stop still proving acceptable.

On a dull day I tend to rate Ektachrome 64 at ISO 50/18°, and Fujichrome 50 at ISO 32/16°. On very bright days I have rated Kodachrome 64 at ISO 80/20° to help with colour saturation, and experiments like these will help you to get to know the real potential of your colour slide film.

High quality colour slides can be spoiled by indifferent processing so where the film is not process paid, make sure that it is developed by a reputable laboratory who show a real concern for quality control and regularly monitor their E6 processing.

The veritable explosion in colour negative films over the last few years offers a tremendous range of film speeds to choose from. The technology of emulsion manufacture is changing all the time and it is mainly aimed at increasing film speed while reducing grain.

Nevertheless the crispest images still come from the slower and intermediate film speeds while the greatest versatility comes from the fastest, but with some loss of contrast. ISO 100 and ISO 400 colour negative films should cope with most of the conditions found on the fells, the ISO 400 films allowing use of the faster shutter speeds needed for telephoto lenses and to give a bigger zone of sharp focus in fine conditions. It will also help you to get photographs that slower films just could not

Great Gable

cope with under dark forbidding skies or at sunset and sunrise.

I do not use much black and white film but when I do, I use Ilford FP4 (ISO 125/22°) developed in Microdol X for 14 minutes. I find that this fairly basic combination gives me the sort of negative contrast that I prefer for publication, coupled with fine grain that can easily cope with the enlargement of even quite small parts of a 35mm negative.

Exposure

All exposure meters, including those built into cameras are calibrated to measure average luminance and provide readings that would render the negative or colour slide with a density equivalent to an 18% grey tone ie. it assumes that every scene reflects about 18% of the light striking it.

This means that the meter sees everything as a medium grey. When you know this, it is not surprising that automatic camera systems often cannot cope with the sometimes quite wide variations in contrast found on the fells of the Lake District.

Most of the time, conditions are not perfect ie. they do not reflect 18% of the light averaged over the entire frame and the landscape photographer has to make adjustments based on how much of a scene is average and how much of it is outside average conditions. The standard middle tone is rarely found among mountains and lakes, where the ratio of bright sky to dark masses often requires substantial amendment of the meter reading.

When confronted with snow for instance, the meter assumes that this is neutral grey in very bright light and will recommend stopping down to get it back to grey again. In this case you need to overexpose the picture by one or two stops to get crisp white, rather than murky grey snow.

Again, if you want a range of black hills against a sombre sky the meter will assume that they are really middle grey in very poor light and recommend an exposure which will bring them back to average ie. it will suggest too much exposure and you will have to underexpose by one or two stops in order to get the effect that you want.

In general you need to remember that if the main area of your picture seems significantly brighter than medium grey you will have to give more exposure than the meter suggests, and if the main area looks significantly darker than medium grey you will have to underexpose to keep the darker mood.

It helps if you know your film and your camera in such a way that the only variables you have to worry about are the lighting conditions that you find when you want to take a picture. Such knowledge leaves you free to look at the light, compensate if necessary, and then concentrate on framing your subject.

Bracketing

One way of ensuring that you come away with a correctly exposed picture is to 'bracket'. Slightly more time and film consuming, this simple technique offers a fail-safe opportunity to get the exposure right under non-average conditions, especially if the cost and effort of getting to where you are far outweighs the cost of a few frames of film.

Set the exposure as you feel it should be, shoot a frame and then expose a frame one stop over and another one stop under, or if you feel confident that the best picture must be either over or underexposed, simply shoot a couple of frames by changing stops in one direction only.

Lenses that allow half a stop adjustments can help you with even finer bracketing options. I always bracket pictures that I feel will be special. I usually keep the shutter speed constant, (I nearly always use the slowest speed compatible with hand-holding anyway), changing the aperture up or down as I feel the situation warrants.

This is not to suggest that you use three or four frames for every photograph you take; you will have to judge when and where this is necessary and trade off the time involved and the cost of film against your need to get the best possible pictures.

Slow Shutter Speeds

My experience of lighting conditions in the UK, especially in the Lakes, is that for most of the year there is not too much of it about. I often find myself in the position of not being able to get a picture at the widest possible aperture with a hand-held shutter speed of 1/60 of a second. This is widely regarded as the slowest shutter speed compatible with hand-holding.

The most obvious answer for this of course is to take a tripod. With a camera firmly supported, and with the aid of a cable release, one can use very slow shutter speeds with small apertures and get all the flexibility that you need under poor lighting conditions. Unfortunately, I discovered very early in my mountain photography that I just could not carry one with everything else that I needed. Obviously at lake and road level it is wise to keep a tripod handy for slow shutter speeds, but on the fells, unless you have someone to carry it for you, or you are very fit, my advice is to leave it at the bottom. It will get heavier as you get higher and if you do not use it, it becomes a resented piece of scrap metal as the day wears on.

This advice will be heresy to many who feel that sharp pictures are only possible with a tripod. My own view, even at road level, is that setting-up a tripod takes too much time and loses much of the spontaneity often necessary to catch good pictures. The 'ever-ready' approach has led me to develop a 'steady-hand' technique which enables me to use shutter speeds slower than 1/60 of a second, and some of the photographs in this book were taken of 1/30, 1/15, 1/8 and even 1/4 of a second while hand-held.

As the light fades, or if the film speed is not fast enough for changing light, or if I want as much of the picture as possible to be within the possible zone of sharp focus, I fall back on this 'steady hand'.

I just hold the camera very tightly against my eye, (if you wear glasses as I do you will have to practise this a bit to get the most firm position) I breathe in, and press the shutter ever so carefully; it works about 70% of the time and gives me some successful pictures, whereas by sticking to the rules, there would be none. So give it a try.

Wide-angle lenses tolerate slower shutter speeds better because detail in the landscape invariably looks smaller within the wide-angle of view, and thus less evidently blurred by any camera movement. Always be particularly suspicious of a meter reading taken through a wide-angle lens; it will inevitably cause the meter to be unduly influenced by the sky leaving the foreground somewhat underexposed.

Lenses and Picture Sharpness

I have already noted the range of lenses that I personally find useful. These include two zoom lenses, which some fastidious photographers would argue can never have the optical quality of single focal length lenses. This may be true under some rigorous test, but the design and optical quality of zoom lenses has improved immensely over the last few years and, as is the way with optical technology, will continue to improve in the future. So I am quite happy to forego the very slight loss of resolving power that I might get with these lenses in order to gain the tremendous advantage of light weight and variable angles of view which this particular design gives me.

The standard lens that most people get with their 35mm SLR camera is often a 50/55 mm lens giving an angle of view between 40° and 50°. These lenses provide a angle of view very similar to the field of vision that you get with the human eye. Standard lenses are usually quite fast ie. they have a maximum aperture that will allow pictures to be taken under poor lighting conditions eg. f/2, f/1.8, f/1.4 etc.

These lenses are handy when you are quite close to a scene, or when you want to include people as an important part of a picture but generally speaking they are not very useful to the landscape photographer. I often find when composing landscape pictures that I need a wider or narrower field of view than that provided by a standard lens, and that I either have to move back or move towards the scene to get exactly the framing that I want. It is obviously a personal idiosyncrasy that standard lenses rarely give me a satisfying composition, and you may well find them very useful for your landscape photographs, all part of developing your own way of 'seeing'.

Wide-Angle Lenses

These lenses range in focal length from around 14mm to 35mm and provide angles of view between 114° and 63°. As well as including so much more of a scene in the viewfinder and on the film, such lenses encourage close viewpoints that lead to more severe perspective than may be obtained with a standard lens. The close viewpoint exaggerates space relationships by expanding the apparent distance between nearby and more distant objects. In this way, a cairn on a mountain summit, or a boulder in a stream, which are close to the camera can seem massive against what seems to be a very distant background, and a path winding its way up the mountain will look longer than it really is. Such effects are not caused by the focal length of the lens but by the close viewpoints involved.

These qualities, if harnessed with care, can lead to some dramatic landscape pictures that bring panorama and power to your photography. Personally, I would not use a lens with a focal length of less than 24mm (angle of view about 84°) for landscape photography. This is because lenses below that focal length will render any detail so small on the film that only massive enlargement will be able to pick out even the most significant features in a landscape and, more important, the problem of wide-angle distortion appears. Features near the corners of the frame become elongated and mishapen.

Another tip here, drawn from painful experience of spoilt pictures, is to beware the use of square

universal filter holders on wide-angle lenses. If you are not careful, the angle of view may well include the corners of the filter holder, perhaps only just visible in the corners of the frame under bright light, but lost under darker conditions, causing vignetting at each corner of your final photograph. To avoid this, carefully follow the filter holder manufacturer's instructions with regard to wide-angle lenses; you may find that those holders designed for larger format cameras are also available in sizes that fit these lenses without causing the vignette effect.

One of the great advantages of the wide-angle lens is its big depth of field ie. more of the scene is within the zone of sharp focus than is possible with a standard or telephoto lens. This is particularly useful when you want to include sharply defined detail in the near foreground.

The question of depth of field is important to the landscape photographer because it is very rare that elements of a landscape photograph are required to be out of focus. Occasionally a particular composition might look more interesting if it is framed by say the branch of a tree which can itself be less sharp than the rest of the picture, drawing attention to the crisp rendering of the rest of the scene, but generally a sharp photograph from front to back is what is wanted.

When focusing on a particular point, say for example a tree, using a particular lens aperture, there will be an area in front of the tree that is in focus, and an area behind it that is also in focus, from the front to the back of these areas is a zone of sharp focus and this is known as 'the depth of field'. The smaller the aperture that you are able to use on your camera, eg f/11, f/16 and f/22, the greater this zone of acceptable sharpness is, the larger the aperture, eg f/1.8, f/2.8, f/4, the less it will be. Another useful point to remember is that irrespective of the aperture used, there is always more of the area in focus behind your main subject than in front of it, so if you focus at some point just beyond your main subject, the subject itself may not be picked out sharply.

There is usually a depth of field scale on the barrel of most modern SLR lenses, marked off in f/

Skiddaw perfectly reflected in Derwentwater

numbers and careful reading of the manufacturer's instructions will tell you how to make the best use of it. Depth of field improves as the camera-to-subject distance increases, and thus for most landscape situations there is a built-in depth of field advantage.

Hyperfocal Distance

In order to get the best possible sharpness from a lens, the maximum depth of field should always be utilised. This is often not achieved because many photographers assume that the lens must always be focused at infinity. This is not the case, indeed it is wasteful of focusing power because depth of field extends on both sides of the point of focus.

To reclaim some of the foreground we need to focus the lens at a point closer than infinity and the best point on which to focus is the hyperfocal distance. When your lens is set at infinity the hyperfocal distance is the distance between the camera and the closest point of acceptable sharpness for the aperture set. For example, if you are using an aperture of f/8 and you focus at infinity, and for the sake of this exercise the 12ft numeral on the distance scale is opposite f/8 on your depth of field scale, then you re-focus at 12ft. Everything will now be in focus from *half* the hyperfocal distance ie. 6ft to infinity, extending your zone of acceptably sharp focus much closer to the camera than was the case with the lens simply focused on infinity.

As you change the lens aperture, so the hyperfocal distance changes. Another way to achieve this

quickly, is to set the infinity mark on the distance scale to the number on the depth of field scale that corresponds with the aperture you are using, ie opposite f/8 in the above example.

Telephoto Lenses

The primary purpose of a telephoto lens is to bring subjects closer and make them relatively larger. In landscape photography this means using the narrow angle view to pick detail out of the larger scene and framing it so that it fills the picture. Focal lengths of telephoto lenses range from about 80 mm to 600 mm, there are some of longer focal length eg 800 mm and 1000 mm but these are extremely expensive and very heavy to carry around. Due to the increased image size and because telephoto lenses are quite heavy, it is very important to avoid camera shake and a subsequent blurred image. One rule of thumb is to use a camera shutter speed roughly equal to the focal length of the lens that you are using eg a shutter speed of 1/125 of a second for a 135 mm lens, a shutter speed of 1/250 for a 200 mm lens etc. The 'steady hand' technique is very important here and, using a zoom telephoto that covers 70mm - 250mm, I often hold the camera *and* the lens, gripping the latter as near to the camera body as possible. Again these are techniques that you need to explore for yourself. Everyone I talk to has slightly different preferences to myself. Obviously being able to pull-in detail from some miles away is a great advantage to the landscape photographer, but care is needed. Telephoto lenses have a very shallow depth of field even at the smallest aperture and the longer the focal length the shallower the depth of field so accurate focusing is very important. Sometimes this shallow depth of field is useful in allowing you to isolate some detail or feature from a distracting scene allowing it to stand out sharply from a diffused background. Telephoto lenses used from distant viewpoints also seem to compress the distance between foreground and background, distant hills or mountains will appear much bigger in relation to a house or a church in the foreground, and a receding pathway will be shortened with the result that the features along it will seem much closer together. Many telephoto lenses, and particularly the zoom variety, are quite slow ie. they do not have a very wide maximum aperture, at best often f/3.5, f/4 or f/5.6 and this can be a disadvantage in dim light that only fast film or the use of a tripod can overcome.

Whatever lenses you use, the idea is to choose the one most appropriate to the scene before you. Remember that you also control the field of view by moving forward or backwards to get the best composition. This may well mean moving away from the established footpaths which often run over the centre of wide ridges and complicate picture taking by being too far from the edge of a slope or a cliff. Obviously a commonsense concern for safety at all costs must prevail on the fells, but sensible movement away from footpaths is often necessary if you are to avoid too much distracting foreground. Pathways that roll gently away downhill can be a useful foreground device in a picture, stressing distance and perhaps carrying the viewer towards the main feature, but this is not always the case and the search for the 'end' of a particularly gentle summit, such as that on Catbells or the track from Rosthwaite to Watendlath may require considerable movement away from the footpath in order to eliminate distracting tufts of grass.

Obviously this is more of a problem with wide-angle lenses than with lenses of standard or telephoto focal lengths, but then it is often the wide-angle lens that provides the expanse needed for a powerful landscape photograph. Remember that foreground detail can provide a vast landscape with a sense of scale; people, rocks, houses, tumbling streams can, if chosen carefully, give interesting depth to a landscape photograph, and whatever sort of lens you are using, you are in control - try the picture with the foreground, try it without, if you have a zoom lens ring the changes by viewing the scene at various focal lengths; no lens ever made a decision as to what was or was not to be included in a picture. That is your challenge and eventually becomes your way of seeing.

Filters

There is probably nothing so personal in a photographer's gadget bag as the sort of filters that he or she will prefer to use. This is my choice.

Ultra-Violet

I always keep a circular screw-in ultra-violet (UV) filter attached to all of the lenses that I use. These virtually colourless filters need no exposure compensation, and are designed to remove the ultra violet rays which are invisible to the human eye, but to which all emulsions are sensitive. Ultra violet light abounds in mountainous areas, near the sea, amongst snow, near large patches of water and under clear blue skies. It causes excessive blue to be shown on the film if not eliminated.

These filters also reduce the atmospheric haze that might partially obscure the distant part of a scene. This haze is due to light being scattered by particles in the atmosphere which cause a sort of fine mist. Because ultra violet light has short wavelengths, it is more easily scattered, and the haze becomes greatly exaggerated by the film emulsion. All colour values become increasingly weak towards the horizon as these particles dilute both colour and the detail in the scene. These filters are often called 'haze' filters by some manufacturers and photographers in order to emphasise this haze-reducing quality.

It stands to reason that if features in a scene are not directly illuminated by the sun, their only source of illumination is the blue of the sky itself, and thus clear skies will contain a lot of scattered blue or ultra-violet light.

I keep UV filters on my lenses to help solve these problems, and to protect the soft glass of the lenses against scratches, dust and moisture. All my equipment gets rough handling at times during the scrabble to match camera bodies and lenses, so I let the UV filters take the wear. This is a contentious point as scratches and chips on the filter surface can have an adverse effect on image sharpness and contrast and these can show up on the film, particularly when shooting against the light eg. at sunset. Also soiled and greasy filter surfaces can cause flare; the moral is to keep your filter surfaces spotlessly clean, replacing them if they get scratched too badly, and to use an appropriate lens hood.

A similar effect to the UV filter is obtained by

using a skylight filter, this is often tinted a very pale pink but needs no exposure compensation. You may also come across a group of filters called 'warm-tone'. These have various degrees of amber colour and again they help suppress blue casts in overcast conditions and on subjects lit by bright blue sky. They often correspond to Kodak Wratten filter numbers, 81, 81A, 81B and 81C, and can literally be used to 'warm-up' a scene.

Polariser

A more advanced text than this will tell you why a polariser works as it does. All I want to explain here is what it looks like, what it can achieve and how to handle it so that you get the most benefit from it. Firstly, it looks slightly grey and it is in fact quite dense. It will absorb some light and, therefore, it will require exposure increases of up to one and a half stops to achieve a correct exposure. Most camera metering systems can cope with polarising filters and give a correct reading through the filter. Some, however, get confused by it and you will have to discover if your camera is one of these. If it is try looking out for a circular polariser which should work better with it.

To work properly a polarising filter has to be able to rotate in front of the lens and if it is the screw-in type then this mechanism is usually built-in to the filter mount. If it is a square filter you will have to rotate the holder to get the desired effect.

One of its effects is to darken blue skies, accentuating the white cloud patterns so that the scene looks much more dramatic without affecting the colour balance. When viewing a scene through the lens of an SLR with a polariser attached you can see the changes to the contrast of a scene come and go as you rotate the filter. Two conditions are necessary to get this effect; first it must be a bright sunny day - no sun, no polarised light and, therefore, no effect - and, second, maximum contrast occurs only when the part of the sky seen in your viewfinder is at right angles to the sun. This means that when the sun is directly overhead, light from the entire horizon is polarised; as the sun goes down the band tilts so that at sunrise or sunset it forms an arch with its apex directly above you. By rotating your polariser slowly you will be able to see if all the sky in the frame will darken or whether you need to change your position. Do not keep a polariser on the front of your lens all the time, there may well be skies that you do not want to darken. Also be wary of using it when the sun and sky are not at 90° to each other, sometimes this can give an interesting effect but all too often you will have a photograph badly unbalanced by quite sharp gradations of dark and light sky. Also take care when fitting any sort of filters to wide-angle lenses, even the rim of a circular screw-in type may just be included in the len's angle of view causing vignetting.

A polarising filter is also useful for eliminating or reducing reflections from non-metallic surfaces. Obviously this can be useful for suppressing surface reflections on lakes, tarns, and rivers, but it only works when the angle between the camera and the water's surface is about 35°. Again, you have the control if you use an SLR, by rotating the filter slowly you can see the extent to which the reflections are removed. Of course, you may not want to suppress all the reflections from a sheet of water, sometimes a dark, clear tarn or lake can look spectacular against the rest of a scene; at other times the effect of removing all the reflections from water can seem dull and lifeless so this facility needs to be used with some care. Under certain conditions a polariser can also help improve the saturation of colours. It does this by eliminating surface reflections from objects or features in a scene and again you need to be at an angle of about 35° to the object for it to work effectively. In landscape photography you will be surprised just how strong foreground greens and autumn colours can become by using a polariser in this way.

Polarising filters are quite expensive, especially the larger screw sizes, but they are invaluable to the landscape photographer. If you use a square filter system you will be able to use a polariser in conjunction with other special effects filters to increase the range and mood of your photography.

Special Effects Filters

A quick flick through the pages of any filter manufacturer's catalogue will reveal the tremendous range of special effects filters that are now on offer, especially from square filter collections. I use some of these as they can be quite valuable in enhancing the mood of what might otherwise be a dull or bland picture, especially in giving impact to winter skies that would often looked washed out or plain white without a touch of added colour. The argument for keeping it all natural and avoiding any intrusion of artificial colour or effect has never bothered me as the way I want to see the scene is more important to me than the way it is.

I am particularly fond of graduated filters. These are designed to filter one part of the scene while not filtering another, the different densities merging gradually, hence the name. These filters can be coloured or of a neutral grey density, this latter variety help to equalise the exposure differences between say a bright sky and a darker foreground while the coloured filters can add impact and interest to skies that would otherwise have none. My favourite coloured graduates are tobacco, blue, pink and grey, roughly in that order. Their effect can be very striking and dramatic when used with wide-angle lenses at small apertures, and more subtle and pastel-like when attached to telephoto lenses at larger apertures. They can be combined with each other in almost infinite permutations, in similar positions or with the densities opposed. My advice is to settle on a particular manufacturer's range and experiment, remembering that as you pile on the filters, less light reaches the film, and apertures need to be wider and shutter speeds slower to cope with the extra light absorption. I occasionally use a simple four-star filter or a cross screen that produces a four-pointed star when pointed at strong highlights in a scene, in my case this is usually when I am shooting directly into the sun.

I have also experimented with one or two different diffusers which have little effect on the sharpness of a scene but which can soften a landscape without suppressing too much detail. Depending on their density these filters spread the highlights and reduce contrast in the picture, sometimes, not always, giving a quite pleasing result. A pastel filter used on back-lit subjects can also have an attractive and delicate effect especially when used in a forest or where lines of trees stand against the light.

I get by with these filters in conjunction with the films and lenses that I have mentioned. They do not work every time, but I am comfortable with the sorts of results that they give me, and like you, I will continue to try out new developments and features as they appear on the market, and, if they work for me, gradually integrate them into my way of doing things.

The great joy of photography on the fells is the infinite range of lighting and weather conditions that you find there. In the end, no advice can take the place of your own, gradually assimilated experience. Take note of what you see and how you see it, and if you fail to make a good photograph at any time, try and work out why, then go back and have another go.

Personal Equipment

For those readers who are interested in the precise specifications of the equipment that I have used for the photographs in this book, I list them below.

These items of equipment are my personal choice, and as I have noted elsewhere, you will need to investigate your own needs carefully reconciling your budget with factors like ease of handling, specification and portability.

I use two Canon SLR bodies, the multi-mode A1 and the AE1 Program; I usually use the A1 for colour photgraphy and the AE1 for black and white work, occasionally switching them around as circumstances change.

I generally keep my 50mm f/1.8 standard lens on the camera with the black and white film in and swop lenses around as I require.

I also use a Sigma 70mm – 250mm f/3.5-f/4.5 zoom lens, a Sigma 28mm – 85mm f/3.5 zoom lens, and a Sigma 24mm f/2.8 wide angle lens.

As well as this 35mm equipment I also use a Mamiya 645 1000S single lens reflex camera with a PD prism, this gives me a frame size of 6cm × 4.5cm. The standard lens for this camera is 80mm f/2.8, the wide-angle lens that I use with it is 45mm f/2.8, and the telephoto lens that I have is the 210mm f/4.

Further Reading

The author would like to acknowledge the value of the books noted below, which together with personal observation and conversation with many Cumbrians, have helped in developing the background information on the locations used by Hugh Walpole in his Herries Chronicle.

WALKING GUIDES

Davies, Hunter
A Walk Around the Lakes, Weidenfeld and Nicolson, 1979 (Hamlyn Paperback, 1980).

Ordnance Survey
Lake District, O.S. Leisure Guide, 1" × 2½"
Maps Used in Book Form, 18 Planned Walks, 1984.

Wainwright, A.
A Pictorial Guide to the Lakeland Fells,
Book Four, The Southern Fells, 1960.
Book Five, The Northern Fells, 1962.
Book Six, The North-Western Fells, 1964.

Wainwright, A.
Fellwalking with Wainwright,
Michael Joseph, 1984.

GENERAL

Bragg, Melvyn
Land of the Lakes, Secker and Warburg, 1983.

Bragg, Melvyn
My Favourite Stories of Lakeland,
Butterworth, 1981.

Burden, Vera
History, People and Places in the Lake District,
Spurbooks Ltd, 1976.

Frazer, Maxwell
Companion into Lakeland: the Folklore Customs and History of the Lake District, Spurbooks, 1973.

Griffin, A. H.
A Year in the Fells: Pages from a Country Diary, Robert Hale, 1976.

Griffin, A. H.
Freeman of the Hills, Robert Hale, 1978.

Knowles, Arthur
Lakeland Today, Robert Hale, 1973.

Lefebure, Molly
Cumbrian Discovery, Victor Gollancz, 1977.

Lefebure, Molly
Cumberland Heritage, Victor Gollancz, 1970. (Arrow Books, 1974; very informative on the graphite mining at Seathwaite).

Lowther, Tom (Rev)
The Parish of Borrowdale with Grange, 1977.
(1981 ed. by Rev Ronald Johns).

Marshall, J. D.
Portrait of Cumbria, Robert Hale, 1981.

Mee, Arthur
The Lake Counties: Cumberland, Westmorland,
fully revised by Gordon Wood, Hodder and
Stoughton, 1969.

Millward, R. and Robinson, A.
Cumbria: Landscapes of Britain, Macmillan,
1972 (very good on the social and economic
structure of the Lake District).

Mitchell, W. R.
Wild Cumbria, Robert Hale, 1978.

Monkhouse, F. J.
The English Lake District, Geographical
Association, 1960.

Nicholson, Norman
Portrait of the Lakes, Robert Hale 2nd ed. 1972.

Orrell, Robert
Saddle Tramp in the Lake District,
Robert Hale, 1979.

Parker, John
Cumbria, John Bartholomew, 1977.

Poucher, W. A.
The Lake District, Constable, 1982. (wonderful
photographs of the area, an inspiration to any
would-be mountain photographer).

Rice, H. A. L.
Lake Country Towns, Robert Hale, 1974.

Rollinson, W.
Life and Tradition in the Lake District,
J. M. Dent, 1974.

Sutton, Shelagh
The Story of Borrowdale, Borrowdale Womens
Institute, 1960.

Spencer, Brian
A Visitors Guide to the Lake District, Moorland
Publishing, 1983.

Unsworth, Walt.
The High Fells of Lakeland, Robert Hale, 1972.

Wilberforce, William
*Journey to the Lake District from Cambridge
1779* ed. by C. E. Wrangham, Oriel Press.

Wordsworth, Dorothy
Journals ed. by Mary Moorman, OUP 1971.

Acknowledgements

Many kind people have had a part in putting this book together. Space limits the number that can be recognised here, but I hope that all those who have helped in any way, enjoy the end-product, happily take a share in any credit, and quite naturally remain blameless for any faults.

I would like to thank; Peter Wolfe of Wolfe Medical Publications Ltd., for his help and advice when I needed it most; Ingrid Ryder for her early encouragement and for typing the first draft; Alan Mounsey of Grange-in-Borrowdale for sharing his knowledge of Hugh Walpole, and for permission to reproduce the black and white photograph of Walpole; Doctor and Mr. Watter of Brackenburn for their courtesy and help, similarly to Mr. and Mrs. Holden of Brackenburn Lodge; Sir Rupert Hart-Davis for kindly reading an early draft of the introduction; Mr. Norman Gandy, Curator of the Fitzpark Museum, Keswick, whose dry humour was companion to my study of the Walpole manuscripts; Trefor Hughes-Jones for accompanying me over some of the highest points in the Herries compass; George Wakefield for his help on technical matters and for his fastidious reading of the text; Judith Price for patiently dealing with the amendments involved in typing the final manuscript; Grant Bradford for his critical and sensitive approach to the design of the book; Andrew Boss for his work on the maps; Harry Ricketts my publisher for his invaluable help and guidance in getting the arrangement and format right; and last but by no means least to Yvonne Kane, companion and critic, supporter and sustainer.

In addition the author and publishers would like to thank Macmillan, London and Basingstoke for permission to quote from the four Herries novels, Rogue Herries, Judith Paris, The Fortress and Vanessa.

Yvonne Kane

Trevor Haywood

A lecturer and freelance photographer, Trevor Haywood is closely associated with the English landscape, his extensive library of scenic and landscape photographs feature regularly in books, magazines, travel brochures and advertising.

His feature work for several quality illustrated journals is well known and this his first book is the culmination of his landscape and conservation work over the last five years.

His highly original interpretation of the landscape of Hugh Walpole's Herries novels is built on many months spent in the northern lakes observing their moods in all seasons and types of weather.

Trevor Haywood lives in Kidderminster, Worcestershire.